CENTRE FOR EDUCATIONAL RESEARCH AND INNOVATION

Schooling for Tomorrow

Demand-Sensitive Schooling?

EVIDENCE AND ISSUES

OECD

ORGANISATION FOR ECONOMIC CO-OPERATION AND DEVELOPMENT

ORGANISATION FOR ECONOMIC CO-OPERATION AND DEVELOPMENT

The OECD is a unique forum where the governments of 30 democracies work together to address the economic, social and environmental challenges of globalisation. The OECD is also at the forefront of efforts to understand and to help governments respond to new developments and concerns, such as corporate governance, the information economy and the challenges of an ageing population. The Organisation provides a setting where governments can compare policy experiences, seek answers to common problems, identify good practice and work to co-ordinate domestic and international policies.

The OECD member countries are: Australia, Austria, Belgium, Canada, the Czech Republic, Denmark, Finland, France, Germany, Greece, Hungary, Iceland, Ireland, Italy, Japan, Korea, Luxembourg, Mexico, the Netherlands, New Zealand, Norway, Poland, Portugal, the Slovak Republic, Spain, Sweden, Switzerland, Turkey, the United Kingdom and the United States. The Commission of the European Communities takes part in the work of the OECD.

OECD Publishing disseminates widely the results of the Organisation's statistics gathering and research on economic, social and environmental issues, as well as the conventions, guidelines and standards agreed by its members.

Also available in French under the title:
L'école face aux attentes du public
Faits et enjeux

Foreword

Many identify a critical shift from traditional schooling towards the future to lie in the move from "supply-led" systems – operating to procedures decided by educational authorities, schools and teachers – towards systems which are much more sensitive to "demand". But, whose demands should these be? Do we know what the evidence reveals about the attitudes and expectations of parents and students, who are arguably those with greatest stake in what goes on in schools? How well do schools currently recognise these demands? Is the promotion of responsiveness to the wishes of students, parents and their communities a democratic norm or a sign of rampant educational consumerism?

These are among the questions addressed in this latest volume in OECD's "Schooling for Tomorrow" series. It examines and clarifies different aspects of the "demand" concept. It brings forward international evidence to reveal attitudes and expectations. It examines the ways in which demands are expressed in contemporary school systems and especially the room for the exercise of "choice" and "voice". The focus is primarily on parents and students, where evidence is most readily available, while including information on general public opinion, employers, and specific groups in the population. Even with such a focus, this study reveals just how patchy is the available research evidence; it concludes that this is an area ripe for further national and international study.

This publication complements the other volumes in the "Schooling for Tomorrow" series and especially the recent *Personalising Education* report (OECD, 2006). The OECD's Centre for Educational Research and Innovation (CERI) also undertook an earlier study on choice, which resulted in a working paper: "School: A Choice of Directions" (OECD, 2002). Country reactions to that paper helped to shape this study for there was a generalised concern that its complex and controversial subject matter required a more extensive exercise than the approach followed then. Countries were thus invited to participate in the demand study through the nomination of national experts, each preparing a report to a common framework (see Annex). The participating countries were Austria, the Czech Republic, Denmark, England, Finland, Hungary, Japan, Poland, the Slovak Republic and Spain, (plus additional material from the

United States), with reports submitted between mid-2004 and mid-2005 (country reports can be found at: *www.oecd.org/edu/future/sft*).

These are issues of interest not only to CERI in OECD's Education Directorate. The PISA (Programme for International Student Assessment) surveys include attitudinal questions which lead to important insights to complement the more familiar achievement results, some of which have informed the chapters that follow. CERI joined forces with the OECD's Education Committee in organising, together with the education authorities in Flanders, an International Seminar in Brussels in May 2006 on the theme of "Demand, Autonomy and Accountability in Schooling". This seminar discussed the CERI work on demand and provided valuable input for new Education Committee reflections around "Parental Choice, School Autonomy, and System Accountability".

Material from the demand study has already been the subject of a special issue of the *European Journal of Education*, "Attitudes, Choice and Participation – Dimensions of the Demand for Schooling", Vol. 41 No. 1, 2006 (Guest editors: Anne Sliwka and David Istance).

Within the OECD, the "Schooling for Tomorrow" project leader David Istance was responsible for this report, along with Henno Theisens. Delphine Grandrieux and Jennifer Cannon prepared and edited the text for publication. This report is published under the responsibility of the Secretary-General of the OECD.

Anne-Barbara Ischinger
Director for Education

ACKNOWLEDGEMENTS

We would like to acknowledge the important contribution of the national experts and their organisations in providing the basis for this study. We also wish to thank the national authorities for commissioning the reports and permitting their country's participation.

The reports' authors are: Austria, Lorenz Lassnigg (Institute for Advanced Studies, Vienna); the Czech Republic, Jiří Kotásek (Ministry of Education, Youth and Sports), David Greger and Ivana Procházková (Charles University, Prague); Denmark, Peter Ulholm (KLEO, Centre for Competence, Leadership, Evaluation of Organisational Development, Copenhagen); England, Wendy Keys (Independent Consultant); Finland, Kari Nyyssölä (Finnish National Board of Education); Hungary, Judit Lannert, György Mártonfi and Irén Vágó (National Institute for Public Education, Budapest); Japan, Akira Ninomiya (Hiroshima University); Poland, Andrzej Janowski and Danuta Uryga (Maria Grzegorzewska Academy of Special Education, Warsaw); the Slovak Republic, Peter Plavcan (Ministry of Education); and Spain, Liliana Jacott and Antonio Maldonado (Universidad Autonoma de Madrid).

David Plank, Michigan State University provided the report presenting the US evidence and the clarification of the demand concept which made an important input to Chapter 1. Anne Sliwka, University of Trier, Germany prepared the initial synthesis of the large corpus of country material. Both have made an invaluable intellectual contribution throughout the project.

We wish to thank the Department of Education and Training, Flemish Community of Belgium, for hosting the International Seminar on "Demand, Autonomy and Accountability in Schooling" in Brussels, May 2006. This was made possible by Gaby Hostens and his team, as well as the support of the Minister Frank Vandenbroucke and Head of Cabinet Dirk van Damme. We wish to acknowledge the input made by members of the "Schooling for Tomorrow" network at different stages of the work and by the CERI Governing Board in discussing an earlier draft in November 2005.

Table of Contents

Executive Summary

The concept of "demand" applied to education

Demand has quickly become an established part of the discourse on educational reform across the world. It is a controversial concept. For some, it is about rectifying an excessively bureaucratic approach to education ("supply-driven" systems), but this can quickly be associated with the precepts of New Public Management – an increased role for clients and markets, even privatisation, which for many is at odds with the traditional aims of education to promote equity, cultivate humanity, and sustain local communities.

Demand is also an important concept. It takes a prominent position in the reform debates in many OECD countries, whether to enhance participation and active forms of personalised teaching and learning or to improve public services through the pressures of quasi-markets. It is thus a broad concept, leaving it open to multiple interpretations in developing reform agendas. It is because demand is controversial and important but difficult to pin down that a systematic clarification is needed of both the concept and associated empirical evidence.

The launching point for the report is that demand is a multi-dimensional concept that needs to be unpacked. There is clarification of the ways in which it can be expressed (exit and voice) and the potential impacts a more demand-led system may have for such key aims as quality and equity. There are both collective and individual levels of demand (see table below). The levels and expressions of demand interact; for example, the demands for specific types of education from particular groups in society (collective voice) promote diversity which enhances individuals' room to choose.

Better understanding the mechanisms for expressing demand and their interactions is not only an important means of understanding contemporary educational developments but it permits a focus on the outcomes resulting from applying these mechanisms in individual schools or systems.

	EXIT	VOICE
INDIVIDUAL	Individuals choosing and changing a school or programme, market choice mechanisms, or leaving altogether such as for home tuition.	Parents or students directly participating in decision-making in schools and having an important role in the learning process (personalisation).
COLLECTIVE	Groups establishing schools – purely private or publicly-funded private – based on particular religious, ethnic, linguistic or pedagogic grounds.	Interest group influence on schooling issues, such as through curriculum consultation, lobbying, pressure group politics.

Some key findings

This study is based on different national reports which synthesise research findings and datasets particular to their countries (the participating countries were Austria, the Czech Republic, Denmark, England, Finland, Hungary, Japan, Poland, the Slovak Republic and Spain, plus additional material from the United States). In practice this means that there are many blanks in the evidence base as countries do not collect systematic evidence on attitudes, expectations, or satisfaction, whether of parents, employers or the public at large. Though this limits the comparability of the findings, this review has shown the value of exploring this area and of making the evidence base more robust.

Public and parental perceptions of schooling

The evidence available on satisfaction shows a generally positive level of reported satisfaction by the public and parents: there is a stronger belief in the value and achievements of schooling than might be expected. In evidence reported for this study, education is a high public priority alongside health and higher than many other calls on the public purse.

Another generally positive endorsement is the "rule" that the *closer* people are to schooling provision or the education system – the more direct their experience of it – the more satisfied they tend to be about it. This manifests itself in several ways: parents with children going to school are on average more satisfied with schooling than other parents; those who are involved in school governance are more satisfied than other parents; women (who are more likely to participate in school life) tend to be more satisfied than men.

There are other differences related to satisfaction. Across different countries, for instance, the more educated express lower satisfaction with schooling than less educated parents. They are more critical. Parents in urban areas are less satisfied than parents in rural areas, partly because they have higher educational attainment and are more critical, partly because of problems in urban areas.

Parental choice and diversity of provision

This report has prominently used the conceptual distinction between choice (exit) and participation in decision-making (voice) as different ways for parents to express their perceptions of schooling which influence the schooling their children receive. The study shows that countries are moving towards creating and permitting greater parental choice:

- In the countries studied, parents have acquired growing entitlements to choose the school they consider most appropriate for their children. Most often this takes the form of allowing parents to send children to a school outside their own school district. This tends not to be an absolute freedom, where schools can choose which children to accept and they often give preference to students from their own district.

- There is a parallel trend towards greater diversity in the schools on offer. Decentralisation and school autonomy encourage the development of specific school profiles which has been encouraged by policy in some countries. Greater competition supports this trend. Diversity goes further when it means a greater range of types of schools to choose from.

- The information available to parents to make their choices has improved as well. Policy has in general sought to make schooling systems more transparent. School profiles, sometimes including results on national tests, are more generally available to the public and parents.

Though the general trend is to expand the possibilities for choice, not all individuals are responding to this in the same way. The better-educated parents are more likely to exercise deliberate choice. There remain significant differences between urban and rural areas, in part for the simple reason of the greater number of schools to choose from in urban areas.

Parents and community "voice" in schools

There is also a trend from centralised state administration of schooling towards more autonomous schools and increased stakeholder, especially parental, participation in decision-making. These formal opportunities do not always translate in actual influence, however, for a number of reasons:

- Parents are not always aware of the possibilities they have to influence schools and some are simply not interested.

- Another barrier to parents raising their voice is the fear that if they raise critical issues about schooling this might negatively affect their child.

- With a trend towards greater consumerism, some parents will prefer to choose than to invest heavily in a given school.

- In some countries, establishing a school council requires initiative and active participation of parents rather than being set up automatically.

Limited parental participation in school decision-making is compounded by the fact that the parents who do tend not to be a representative sample of the parent body as a whole.

What do students say?

The patchy knowledge base on the demand dimension is particularly problematic regarding students. The basic information on students reveals several general tendencies on reported satisfaction:

- Students are fairly satisfied with school in general, although older students less than younger ones.

- Students in higher tracks are more positive than students in lower tracks.

- Girls tend to be more positive about school than boys.

Where there are complaints, they are most often that school is "boring", or more particularly too many lessons are not interesting enough. According to what students say, the quality of the teaching, the personalisation of methods, and the interest of content make a critical difference. The evidence concerning how dislike of lessons, even a particular lesson, can be telling for the vulnerable to become more permanently detached warrants particular attention: a relatively small but negative experience can have lasting consequences.

In terms of *choice*, in secondary education, most systems have created provisions allowing students to choose between different subjects taught in addition to the compulsory part of the school curriculum but the opportunities for students to raise their *voice* are limited in almost all countries. Formal opportunities for involvement in school decision-making are limited in most countries and where these opportunities exist they are often seen as ineffective.

Selected issues arising

Choice may stimulate quality, but with risks for equity

This report confirms that better educated, middle-class parents are more likely to avail themselves of choice opportunities and send their children to the "best" school they can find. This can increase inequalities by widening the gaps between the sought-after schools and the rest. Inequalities widen too because when the most critical parents take their children from the local school, it loses the critical resource of those who tend to be the movers and shakers, *i.e.* those with most effective voice for improvement from within. The equity argument in favour of transparent choice, on the other hand, is when this means extending to all the same room to choose as privileged parents have always exercised, implicitly or explicitly. In addition, there are the familiar quality arguments in favour of creating greater choice as a vehicle for stimulating improvement. When choices exist, schools must then look beyond their own walls at what others – their potential "competitors" – are doing; without some room for exit to be exercised, parents and students have no threat to back up voice.

A lack of opportunity for voice is the rule, not the exception; but parents do not seem to be clamouring for an intensive involvement in running schools

There are plenty of examples in this report to suggest that a lack of opportunity for external voice to be heard is the norm not the exception. This can reinforce itself as low parental involvement feeds negative views from the education side that parents and the community should have only a very limited say in what goes inside schools, who rightly perceive that schooling is not open to external influence. But there does not seem to be any signs that parents are clamouring to run schools themselves, except in extreme cases of exit (such as home schooling). And, those systems where parents already exercise a high degree of voice are likely to be those where there is greatest trust in schools and teachers as the professionals responsible for education. Expanding voice in education is thus more about finding a new balance between supply and demand than about the one displacing the other.

Parents are in general rather satisfied
about their children's' schooling,
raising the question whether they are
the drivers for change

It is commonplace for the same parents and citizens to be positive about their local school and concerned about the state of education in general. Media, public and political dissatisfaction can co-exist with generally positive satisfaction levels among parents and students. The groups who are typically the drivers of change – the educated middle classes – tend both to be less satisfied but also to have done best with the system as it is. Their concerns are thus under-estimated by the overall satisfaction measures but do not necessarily add up to an agenda for radical change, either. In wanting to safeguard educational advantages, educated parents may even be a conservative force; perhaps paradoxically, much "demand" pressure on school systems still comes from national, state or local policy makers on the supply side. On the other hand, group demands based on articulate linguistic, religious or philosophical grounds, as well as the strongly voiced demands from parents of students with special needs, represent pressure for change, often cutting across the standard influence of socio-economic background.

Greater diversity and role for demand
implies more complex governance in
schooling

The enhanced role for demand, and its diversity, place educational authorities in a more complex governance situation. On the one hand, a growing research and knowledge base fosters the expectations that policies should be evidence-informed. On the other hand, the greater room for local decision-making (the supply side) and the growing pressure to recognise diverse demands about what education is for mean that controlled, mechanistic approaches to policy-making becomes less attainable. The expectation of being able to control change grows just as the means to do so move out in many directions, by many stakeholders. The demand dimension is both an expression and a cause of this new complexity.

Serious shortcomings in information relating to the demands of different individuals and groups need to be addressed, if schooling is to be more demand-oriented

This study has highlighted the sketchy nature of the evidence on demand existing as a general rule across countries. If demand is to have an impact on the educational system or on individual schools it will be important to collect information and data more systematically and to use it. There is much to be done to make knowledge about satisfaction more systematic. Going beyond reactions to existing schooling practices means also to understand better the expectations that parents have, what it is they find important, and what they want from schooling. These are more difficult questions to answer, but they are an important means of bolstering the demand side in systems which tend to be "supply-dominated". It will not be enough just to improve knowledge about parent and student expectations; employers, teachers and local communities, for instance, all have important stakes in schools and we could know much more about their voice. Once information is improved, there are then issues about how to enter it effectively into the decision-making process.

Chapter 1
EXPLORING THE CONCEPT OF DEMAND

Responding to demand is rapidly becoming an established part of the discourse on educational reform. This conceptual chapter explores different definitions and coverage of the demand concept, and develops a framework which is used to organise the rest of this publication. The framework locates the concept of demand in the changing historical context of OECD societies. Parents with growing levels of educational attainment increasingly demand more influence over the education their children receive and education systems are coping with increasingly diverse demands. The framework distinguishes between these demands – shaped by their expectations and satisfaction – and the ways in which they are expressed. Such expression becomes manifest either through choice of an alternative (exit) or by making changes through participation in decision-making (voice). Exit and voice can be exercised by individuals or by groups and interests operating at the collective level.

Introduction

The notion of "demand" in schooling is now in common currency in the educational policy world. Many identify a critical shift of debate and reform from traditional models of the past to dynamic ones of the future to be defined by the change from "supply-dominated systems" towards more demand-sensitive arrangements. This characterisation of shifts from the schooling of yesterday to that of tomorrow makes this a subject ripe for exploration as part of the OECD/CERI "Schooling for Tomorrow" programme. But what does "demand-driven" mean in practice? Is it more than a facile slogan? As this chapter shows, a family of terms and developments related to demand – choice, personalisation and individualisation – are some of the most important, as well as controversial, aspects of education today. There is need to clarify these different concepts and their relationships. This publication complements another recently published in the "Schooling for Tomorrow" series on "personalising education" (2006a), as part of OECD/CERI's contribution to clarifying issues in the way ahead for schooling.

Demand is a multi-dimensional concept which warrants further exploration. Once these dimensions start to come into focus, they should be subject to empirical analysis in order to move beyond abstraction and ideology. This publication is the result of such empirical review; it brings together analytical work in the form of national case studies from 11 countries.[1] The different availability of information in the countries means, however, that the report's evidence base is patchy. Its purpose therefore is exploratory: it indicates the different dimensions of "demand" and how it operates in very different OECD settings, and in doing so it provides insight into the dynamics at play. It highlights questions for further exploration and research.

The aim of this chapter is to review key ideas and concepts related to demand by way of introduction to the findings generated by this study. It presents a framework for analysis in terms of the interactions between forms and levels of demand, educational supply, context, and the articulation of demand.[2] It also recognises by way of introduction diverse other forms of "demand" which have not been explored in this study.

Different meanings of "demand"

It is useful to recognise at the beginning that there are different usages and reactions to the term "demand" as well as the different components and relationships we seek to clarify in the chapter. Some of these are treated in this report, others are not:

- "Demand" is commonly used in an aggregate sense corresponding to "participation". Often, this usage is associated with "student demand" to refer to the overall outcome of a myriad decisions relating to demand, supply and context which end up with a larger or smaller portion of each generation looking to stay on in education or choosing a particular track. So, for example, an increasing participation beyond compulsory schooling is often described as "the growing demand for upper-secondary education".

---

[1] The national case studies were from: Austria, the Czech Republic, Denmark, England, Finland, Hungary, Japan, Poland, the Slovak Republic and Spain, with a separate expert report prepared on the United States.

[2] For this chapter and the framework we are heavily indebted to a paper written by David N. Plank (2005), "Understanding the Demand for Schooling" (see *www.oecd.org/edu/future/sft*)

This study is not about participation in this general sense but the dimensions explored are relevant to understanding better how the "demand" element may well be influencing aggregate participation decisions.

- Another aggregate usage expresses "demand" less in terms of *behaviours* – choices and participation – and more in terms of *rights*. This is typically about "the demand" rather than diverse demands; it is less to be observed or measured but instead to be claimed or asserted. This sense of demand as a human or social right sets the scene (see below) but it is also beyond the scope of this report.

- There is another usage which is not framed as demand *for* (education) but is about its *recognition* through "demand-sensitive" educational arrangements or even "demand-led" systems, as referred to at the beginning of this chapter. This is essentially about process and the "expression of demand" and this is dealt with in this report. Describing schooling as "demand-led", however, begs questions about whose demands are being listened to, to what extent, and what these demands actually are.

- One can distinguish between the *causes/factors* shaping demands and the *demands themselves*. This report is particularly focused on improving our understanding of the latter. But, as recognised in this chapter, there is a philosophical question this raises about how able people are to articulate what they want. Might they want – demand – something else that they haven't yet thought of if it were seriously on offer? We recognise the serious caveats to be made about evidence derived from expressed opinions but also propose that taking stock of knowledge about the demand side through such evidence is an important first step on which to build.

- What is "demand" through one prism can be "supply" through another. Teachers have a myriad demands to make about the aims and conditions of education, which arguably could have been included in this study. We have adopted the position that it would confuse an already-complex subject were the report to include the viewpoints of teachers alongside those of parents, students and the wider public when teachers are more conventionally regarded as part of the supply-side of the educational equation.

There is another reaction framed in the very suitability of the economic terminology of "demand" and "supply" when applied to education, a language which many in education strongly resist. This is an understandable concern from those working within traditions which find this language an alien one. But, such a reaction is not grounds enough to reject such perspectives if it amounts to resistance for reasons of association not substance. Such terminology has become a *lingua franca* in policy analysis, however much some may wish otherwise. To use this *lingua franca* is not about privileging the economic grounds for education over non-economic ones, and indeed "demand" is as much about rights, wishes, and participation as it is about seeking any material benefits which may accrue to educational attainment.

We should also make clear that whilst it is likely – and these are some of the powerful arguments in its favour – that enhanced demand will lead to greater diversity, higher quality and improved responsiveness on the part of institutions and the system, there is no logical necessity that demand be expressed primarily or at all through the standard choice mechanisms which operate for commodities. This study is not based on any presupposition that promoting market or quasi-market mechanisms in education is inherently preferable.

The countries in the case studies underpinning this publication illustrate the wide variety of concepts of "demand" in play and of national policy discourse. This study is about clarifying concepts and relationships informed by evidence, rather than pinning down any elusive notion of "pure" demand. Demand, in short, is a complex concept that needs to be unpacked.

Unpacking a complex concept

No matter how hard we may look, no study can reveal any pure expression of "demand" abstracted from "supply" and context. What people want is closely shaped by what is on offer. And what is on offer and what is asked for both reflect a myriad of influential variables in the environment of schooling and of social and economic life. Moreover, demand needs channels to be expressed; there are different mechanisms to ensure that supply and demand "meet". These mechanisms have different implications – positive advantages and negative costs.

To illustrate the interaction, we can distinguish between demand for *something existing* vs. demand for *something new*. Often people express their demands with regard to an infrastructure that already exists, for example demanding higher standards in science teaching or improved health care in schools. Sometimes – more rarely – the articulation of demand goes beyond what is already in place and calls for the creation of a new educational infrastructure. It takes more imagination to demand something which does not exist, as compared with reacting positively or negatively to something – supply – which already exists. This is further reason why asking people what they want cannot be taken as any pure expression of "demand" as what is wanted tends to be shaped by perceptions of the possible at any one time.

A simple framework of key distinctions and concepts helps us to think about this multi-faceted concept of "demand", as represented in Figure 1.1.

Figure 1.1. Unpacking demand

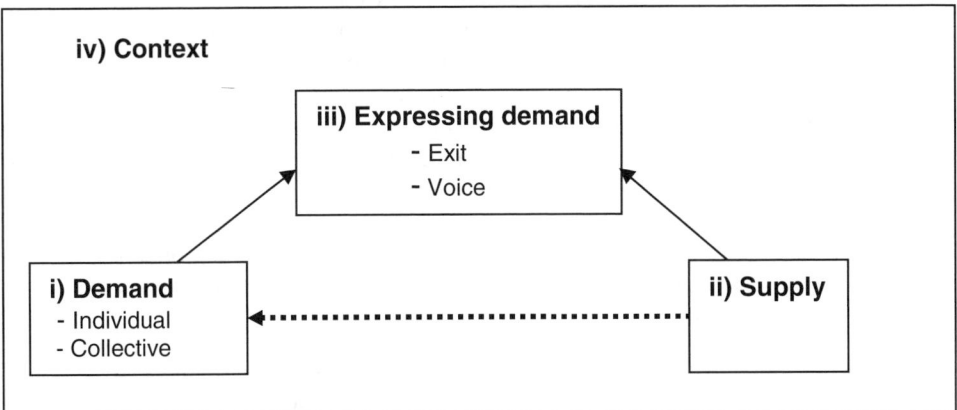

The basic idea underlying this figure is that i) *demand* and ii) *supply* are interacting, mediated by iii) *mechanisms to express demand* and influenced by iv) the *context* in which the interaction takes place. The fact that outcomes are shaped by the mutual influence and tension between these different elements does not diminish the value of focusing on the demand side – the focus of this report. The focus is especially useful because so much of educational policy analysis is either about *supply* – teacher knowledge, structures of school systems, resources etc. – or about social, economic or political *context* which shapes it (the knowledge economy, migration, social inequality and so forth). To look at *demand* and its more effective expression is thus contributing to a more balanced, comprehensive framework for policy analysis rather than one dominated by system and, to a lesser extent, context variables.

The elements in Figure 1.1 – context and supply, demand, and expressing demand – are now discussed as part of unpacking this cluster of relationships. The chapter concludes with key questions which have informed this study related to the demand side of the overall picture.

Changing context and the supply-side

The interest in according greater importance to the demand-side is strongly related to the changing context of schooling, especially regarding how this has altered the primacy of the supply-dominated, publicly-provided schooling tradition which has held the stage for most of the twentieth century. The traditional rationale for the public provision of schools was essentially political. Schools were expected to produce citizens, by providing young people with canonical knowledge including familiarity with national languages and civic traditions. The primary function of public education was tutelary, aimed at incorporating young people into the state by fostering civic unity and national homogenisation through the schools. Next to this political rationale an economic rationale existed for the public provision of schooling. Schooling is what economists characterise as a merit good. Unlike most other goods the private consumption of schooling produces external benefits that accrue to the advantage of the broader society. The general diffusion of schooling supports gains in productivity, public health, and economic growth that improve the lives of all citizens, not just those who go to school.

In the latter half of the twentieth century, the critical dynamics in the education system reflected efforts by the state to enhance the supply of schooling, both by increasing access and by improving the quality of education provided. In many countries the public school system traditionally comprised a highly diversified set of educational opportunities, with access to different options dependent on criteria that included measured aptitude or ability along with gender and race/ethnicity. Access to valued outcomes including university enrolment was dependent on participation in the higher status tracks in the education system. Access to these educational opportunities has often been contingent on examination performance, but sometimes on other criteria including race and gender.

The strong focus on the supply side had its origins in the increasingly wide acceptance of a notional right to education. In this context, the state is responsible not only for building schools, but also for ensuring that citizens avail themselves of educational opportunities. Accepting this responsibility, governments around the world have committed vast resources to expanding and improving their public education systems. Over time the number of young people attending school has steadily increased, as previously marginalised or excluded groups (*e.g.* rural children, girls, and the disabled) have been brought from the margins and into the mainstream of public school systems. In a parallel development, the length of time that children and young people spend in school has steadily increased as well. In most OECD countries, the very large majority of young people now complete at least 12 years of schooling. At least 90% are enrolled in age band spanning

14 or more years in Belgium, the Czech Republic, France, Iceland, Japan and Spain. In OECD countries as a whole, a 5-year-old can expect to have 17.4 year of education, based on current enrolment patterns (OECD, 2006c). Inadequate supply nevertheless continues to constrain enrolments in many parts of the world.

Demand was not absent from the traditional conception of schooling, but it was articulated in terms of access to more, better, and higher-status opportunities within the existing system, rather than for alternatives to the regulated opportunities provided by the state. Initially, disadvantaged households and groups have sought to improve their position through the education system, while prosperous and ambitious households have sought to maintain theirs. Where the demand for schooling was weak or absent (*e.g.* in rural and some religious communities), the role of policy has traditionally been to persuade or coerce parents to send their children to school with consequences for equality in the distribution of educational opportunities.

The issue of demand has traditionally not been problematic as long as it is homogeneous and congruent with the state's expectations. In education systems where the state is the monopoly supplier, it generally has expressed itself in terms that are readily compatible with the state's efforts to equalise and standardise educational opportunities. Communities and households demand that the state provide more and better schooling for their children. Those who find themselves excluded or marginalised may seek inclusion and more equal access to educational opportunities. These manifestations of demand are easily managed; indeed, governments themselves often seek to shape and strengthen the demand by families for education. As standards and expectations for minimal educational attainment have risen, the very success of the policy efforts to equalise opportunities has produced new demands as households have sought to ensure that their own children have privileged access to the best schools and programmes. In some countries this has involved strategic investment in real estate; in others, the purchase of elite private education. In other countries, the demand for schooling has found its expression in the shadow education system of cram schools and supplementary tutoring, which thrive on the margins of state control (Bray, 1999). The lengths people will go to in order to enjoy the advantages associated with education draws attention to the question of *why* education is so keenly demanded: it is often not for the learning as a good in itself but for the advantages that are associated with it. We return to this issue below.

There is now a new context in which a combination of individualisation, diversification and increasingly critical citizens has increased the pressure on the state to deliver more diversified public services. This has coincided with two other developments. First, there is the growing belief, now reaching primary and secondary education though in some countries more than others, that public services improve when they are delivered decentralised and in competition. Second, there is the notion now increasingly stressed by educational scientists that putting the young person in the centre of the learning process is more effective than traditional approaches in which the young person is not so much involved as done to. So now critical policy questions arise about how governments should respond to these new demands. To date, their responses to variation coming from the demand side has been ambivalent at best.

The articulation of demand

In recent years, countries around the world have been confronted by the articulation of increasingly differentiated demands on the public school system, which are less easily managed within the constraints of the traditional education system. The school systems underpinning this study have all undergone significant change in recent decades, where parents and students are increasingly seeing schools as service institutions which should be responsive to their demands.

Individual and collective demand

It is valuable to distinguish the demands which come from individual households and families and those which are associated with groups and collectivities. The economics of education has long worked with the distinction between the individual and social demand for education, which has tended to be understood as distinguishing the individual from society as a whole (the broader notion of the demands and interests of the economy, the nation, etc.). In this report, the notion of collective demands is understood in a more sociological sense. It refers to how demand can be articulated by specific interests and groups, for example those based on region, ethnicity, or language, but also by employer organisations, labour unions or political parties. Their demand is for educational policies and practices that better serve the interests of their group.

On an individual level, parents and students have become more demanding, as educational attainment has gone up and individualisation has become more pronounced. Paludan (2006, p. 84) makes the useful distinction between "optimisation demand" and "maximisation demand". The key characteristic of an "optimisation demand" is that, like someone's demand for food, an individual reaches a point where the need has been satisfied and no more can be consumed – any more and that person is worse off, not better. This he contrasts with learning and health where no natural ceilings exist. To let public services reflect demand in this sense entails limitless expenditure well beyond the means even of the most affluent OECD countries. Paludan is referring especially to the individual concepts "learning" and "good health" rather than the social arrangements to cater for them – "education" and "health-care". It may seem uncontentious that we cannot learn too much or be healthy enough, but we can certainly spend too much time in a school or hospital.

Fred Hirsch's 1970s analysis is relevant to the question of limiting the voracious individual demand for education, apart from the sheer scarcity of resources. He identified education as an exemplar of "positional" or "social" goods (to be distinguished from "material" goods), whose value is not absolute but depends on whether others are consuming it, too. An example is the lonely beach, which is idyllic when someone enjoys it alone but the value of which evaporates when everyone else wants to do the same. For "lonely beach" one can substitute, say, a prestigious university qualification: keenly sought after so long as relatively few have one but with far less appeal were it to be on everyone's curriculum vitae. The concept of "positional goods" applies particularly to the social and cultural spheres, where there is a fixed supply; consumer frustration sets in the more that access is democratised. The application of Hirsch's concept to schooling is clear – its value to the individual depends in part on how many others have similar attainments, and education is subject to continually growing participation and widening access. This sets in train a continual demand for more, not because of the absolute benefits it brings but the relative ones. For schooling to be responsive to the demands of individuals may in general be desirable in terms of creating more democratic and effective public services. But, as learning has no natural ceilings to cap demand and as more education is sought in the never-ending pursuit of relative advantage, schooling cannot be "demand-led" without limits.

Similarly, there may be problems in responding to collective demands. These may be in line with the state's education project but equally the articulation of new demands may represent a serious challenge to the accomplishment of the system's educational objectives. In many countries, for example, demands for instruction in local languages and the affirmation of local cultures in the curriculum may advance local autonomy at the expense of the state's nationalising project. Demands for the acknowledgement of religious beliefs and rituals in publicly-supported schools may alienate students who do not share the dominant religion, or foster fragmentation along confessional lines. These new and diverse demands may conflict with the tutelary, nation-building purposes of the public education system, and with the state's economic objectives as well (*e.g.* if religious traditions restrict the educational opportunities available to girls). We are not judging whether the collective demands are valid and which should be heard rather than others; we are pointing to the potential conflicts such diversification of demand can give rise to.

Moreover, the individual and collective dimensions of the demand for schooling may diverge and intersect in a variety of ways, further complicating the problem of how to respond. For example, the corporate demand for local control over schools may conflict with the demand of individual parents for educational opportunities that improve the social and economic prospects of their children. The nature of this dilemma reveals itself over and over again: in debates over the design of school choice policies; in public disputes over the wearing of headscarves and other ostensibly religious symbols in public schools; in controversies over curriculum content in history and science. The authority and legitimacy of state control in the education system can no longer be taken for granted, and the emergence of diverse demands means that many decisions that were once simply ceded to the state are now open to contestation. Both collective and individual demands may be conflicting when certain individuals or groups have other interests and therefore other demands that cannot be logically combined within one school or one system. Employers may have different priorities from parents; highly educated parents may have different demands than parents without formal education. This diversity of demands may be so great that it is impossible to cater for it within one public system.

Expectations and satisfaction

Both for individual and collective notions of demand, there is a further distinction which is helpful in understanding what shapes demand: *expectations and satisfaction* (Figure 1.2). Expectations critically shape what people want from schooling. Expectations can differ in terms of what and how much is expected. Parents for example may be expecting school to provide their children with different skills or they might expect higher quality without expecting changes in the curriculum. Attitudes expressed as satisfaction provides a measure of how well people assess their expectations to have been met: the more radically expectations differ from what has been experienced, the less satisfied will people be.

Figure 1.2. Demand – expectations and satisfaction

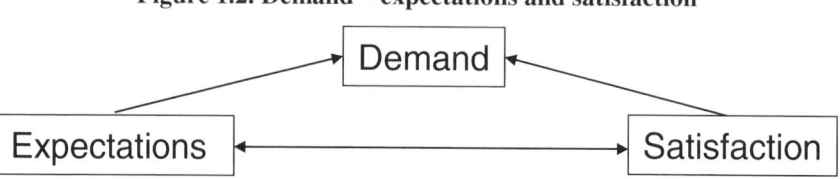

Satisfaction mirrors both reality and expectations. As we will see in the next chapter, middle-class higher-income parents are in general less satisfied with schooling than poorer parents reflecting their higher expectations of what it should achieve. The closer people are to schooling – for example, persons with children at school as compared with employers – tend to be more satisfied as their proximity gives them reason to feel that their expectations have been met. The satisfaction variable is important as dissatisfaction provides an important spur to action and change. Given the contextual trends discussed above, people have clearer expectations than in times gone by and are more demanding about how these should be met.

The expression of demand

Two important mechanisms for expressing demand are *exit* and *voice* (Hirschman, 1970). These concepts have served as key organising precepts for this report. They provide a valuable way of conceptualising behaviour when stakeholders act on their demands to make changes, be it for something different or for something better. That is, they can pursue two alternatives:

- Leave an institution or system in favour of an alternative (*i.e.* exit), or

- Articulate their concerns and become involved in change from within (*i.e.* voice).

School systems to differing degrees offer opportunities for both.

Exit strategies cover a wide range and can look as different as parents selecting a private school for their child or students remaining absent from a class they dislike. Exit strategies can be "horizontal", seeking alternative forms of education or schools based on different belief systems. Or, they can be "vertical" in search of better quality, but with the aims and contents of education not in question. At its most extreme, "exit" means leaving the schooling system altogether: individually this kind of exit may be opting for home tuition – small in most OECD countries but growing in some – or chronic absenteeism; collectively, it means creating new establishments or parallel schooling systems.

Opportunities for voice are provided through political influence on official policy, lobbying and interest group politics. At an individual level it may be through official forms of participation as offered in school or parent councils but also through more informal contacts with schools and teachers.

Both exit and voice can be used collectively or individually as shown in the table below (Table 1.1). This combines the a) individual/collective dimension – who are the stakeholders expressing demand? – with b) their strategies for expressing demand – exit or voice?

Table 1.1. Dimensions and expressions of demand
A matrix of strategies and approaches

	EXIT	VOICE
INDIVIDUAL	Individuals choosing and changing a school or programme, market choice mechanisms, or leaving altogether such as for home tuition.	Parents or students directly participating in decision-making in schools and having an important role in the learning process (personalisation).
COLLECTIVE	Groups establishing schools – purely private or publicly-funded private – based on particular religious, ethnic, linguistic or pedagogic grounds.	Interest group influence on schooling issues, such as through curriculum consultation, lobbying, pressure group politics.

Recent developments in education policy suggest a growing role for exit, and a changing role for voice. Both of these trends pose significant challenges for the traditional, state-centred public education system, where the demand for schooling is assumed to be essentially homogeneous. With parents complaining about schools that fall short of their educational expectations, in a number of countries the policy response to dissatisfaction has been to provide them with alternatives, including charter schools, home schooling, and private schools. This is discussed particularly in Chapter 3. The policy move toward choice reflects a growing reliance on market-type mechanisms as a strategy for addressing public policy problems, and illustrates the growing importance of "exit" in education systems.

However, the development towards greater diversity and greater choice in educational systems is not without costs. For example, decisions by some households to leave particular schools or school districts can reduce the range and quality of educational opportunities provided to the students who remain behind (Fuller, Elmore and Orfield, 1996). Also, as Hirschman argued, it will usually be the clients who care most about quality that will opt to exit the system, meaning that the system is left with a less quality-minded and critical clientele. The lack of critical and (possibly) constructive voice reduces the opportunities for institutional improvement. Finally, greater reliance on the market can reduce the *equity* of the schooling systems. Highly educated parents with more income, in choosing those schools they consider best for their children, are more able to pay the tuition fees charged by schools that offer, say, better facilities or extra-curricular activities. Over time, this can lead to the concentration of children of better-off, better-educated parents in some schools and those of the less well-off and less highly educated in others.

Not creating choice (exit) options can be problematic, too. Without some form of exit possibility, parents and students lack the "muscle" with which to back up voice – threatening exit can lend credibility to strongly-expressed voice. Exit and voice both need to be present in some kind of effective balance. Instead of leaving with the first whiff of dissatisfaction, quality-sensitive parents need to stick with their school and engage in attempts to improve it – in Hirschman's analysis, they need *loyalty*. He maintains that it is loyalty that prevents consumers from exercising immediate exit, using the threat of exit as one forthright strategy for improving the product or the organisation they care about. However, the creation of markets in education has potential risks in this respect: rising consumerism, for instance, might well lead to declining loyalty.

According to Hirschman, the optimal mix of exit and voice is nevertheless elusive. Managers of organisations have a short-term interest in maintaining their own freedom of manoeuvre and therefore in minimising the exercise of both exit and voice. For consumers or members of an organisation, Hirschman concludes that there is a tendency increasingly to neglect the one of these two which is used: "Once members have a slight preference for, say, voice over exit a cumulative movement sets in which makes exit look ever less attractive and more inconceivable. As a result voice will be increasingly relied on by members at a time when management is working hard to make itself less vulnerable to it" (1970, p. 125). This suggests that either voice or exit mechanisms will dominate at any time, but that a switch to or sudden shock with the other may be very effective. For schools, this suggests that there will never be an ideal, steady balance of voice and exit. Both should be available and each may be used to effect as an alternative to the other.

Concluding remarks

Demand has quickly become an established part of the discourse on educational reform across the world. It is a controversial concept. For some it is associated with the precepts of New Public Management – an increased role for clients and markets, even privatisation – which are at odds with the social and humanistic traditions of education to promote equity, cultivate humanity, and sustain local communities. All these senses have a reflection in the broad concept of "demand", whether to seek to improve public services via the pressures of quasi-markets or to enhance participation and active forms of personalised teaching and learning. That enhancing the role of demand takes a prominent position in the reform debates in many OECD countries, while being such a broad elastic concepts, calls a systematic clarification of both the concept and associated empirical evidence. Hence, the value of the exploration in this volume.

The point of departure has been clarification in terms of the ways in which demand can be expressed (exit and voice) and the potential impacts a more demand-led system may have for key issues like quality and equity. Thus demand is understood as a multi-dimensional concept that needs to be unpacked. The dimensions of exit and voice at both the collective and individual levels have been outlined in this chapter. These different levels and expressions of demand interact in complex ways. For example, the demands for special types of education from specific societal groups (collective voice) lead to diversity that allows individuals to choose.

Better understanding the mechanisms for expressing demand and their interactions is not only useful in itself but it also permits a focus on the outcomes resulting from applying these mechanisms at the levels of schools and the school system. Again the relations are complex. Greater voice may be a force pushing schools to deliver relevant and high-quality teaching; it could be a way for privileged parents – with greater influence and a more developed idea of their demands – to dominate school decision-making in favour of their own children. Hence, the value of backing up the theoretical possibilities by recourse to evidence. The following chapters explore these issues by drawing on the results of the country case material, using the framework developed in this chapter to organise the analysis and discussion.

References

Bransford, J.D., A.L. Brown and R. Cocking (eds.) (1999), *How People Learn: Brain, Mind, Experience and School*, Nationale Academy Press, Washington, United States.

Bray, M. (1999), *The Shadow Education System: Private Tutoring and Its Implications for Planners*, UNESCO.

Deci, E.L., R.U. Vallerand, L.G. Pelletier and R.M. Ryan (1991), "Motivation and Education: The Self-determination Perspective", *Educational Psychologist*, Vol. 26 (3–4), pp. 325–346.

Fuller, B., R.F. Elmore and G. Orfield (1996), *Who Chooses, Who Loses? Culture, Institutions, and the Unequal Effects of School Choice*, Teachers College.

Hirsch, D. (2002), "What Works in Innovation in Education, School: A Choice of Directions", CERI Working Paper, OECD/CERI.

Hirsch, F. (1977), *The Social Limits to Growth*, Routledge and Kegan Paul, London.

Hirschman, A.O. (1970), *Exit, Voice, and Loyalty: Responses to Decline in Firms, Organizations, and States*, Harvard, United States.

OECD (2006a), *Personalising Education*, OECD, Paris.

OECD (2006b), *Think Scenarios, Rethink Education*, OECD, Paris.

OECD (2006c), *Education at a Glance: OECD Indicators – 2006 Edition*, OECD, Paris.

Paludan, J.P. (2006), "Personalised Learning 2025", *Personalising Education*, OECD, Paris, Chapter 6.

Plank, D. (2005), *Understanding the Demand for Schooling*, Report to the OECD.

Chapter 2
PUBLIC AND PARENTAL PERCEPTIONS
OF SCHOOLING

Based on the evidence from the countries taking part in this study, this chapter provides insights on how parents and the wider public perceive schooling. The evidence shows that education ranks as a high priority among the public, despite the often negative messages of media coverage. There tends to be greater satisfaction with schooling than might be expected, and the nearer that people are involved – such as parents commenting on their own children's schooling – the higher the satisfaction tends to be. Dissatisfaction is voiced more by the parents with higher educational attainment and by urban parents compared with their rural counterparts. Different individuals and groups have demanding, not necessarily compatible expectations, giving schools the problem of accommodating these different agendas. If schooling is to become more "demand-led", educators and policy makers should know more about people's expectations; this review shows the value of understanding perceptions of schooling and suggests the need to strengthen the evidence base.

The perception of schooling by different stakeholders provides important indications of how well policy and provision respond to different demands. It provides critical insight into how choices are made and voices exercised in education. Analysing those perceptions thus helps to clarify what demands actually are, how stakeholders express them, and whose are actually being taken into account. Which groups remain silent and what are the reasons for them not giving voice for their demands? Are they satisfied with the current provision of education? How well is their "voice" getting through to the media, the wider public, and to policy makers? In providing insights on these questions, the country reports on which this study is based are mostly focused on parental perceptions while providing some insights on more general public reactions (which are discussed first).

This chapter brings together information from the case study countries on perceptions and attitudes. This was the subject of OECD scrutiny in the 1990s as part of the international indicators programme (INES, see OECD, 1995). Given the subjective basis of the data, it is a complex area in which to produce international comparative indicators. At the national level, several systems (such as Austria, Denmark and Finland among the case study countries), have organised surveys to monitor the viewpoints of various groups of stakeholders. Feedback from these surveys is then intended to inform educational policy-making. How and how far this process of informing policy with evidence about attitudes is actually done is a moot question when a system purports to be "demand-led". An aspect of responding to "voice" might well be taking direct account of opinion about what is judged to be important in education and about how well the goals held by people are being achieved. The question arises then about how evidence about attitudes is actually taken on board in different OECD countries as well as what its appropriate contribution should be.

Schooling in the public eye

The countries in this study vary in the extent to which demand is used in the public debate in different countries. The thrust of the debate is not always the same. In Denmark and Finland, they have focused on equity questions with a broad consensus that relative uniform provision best serves the needs of children growing up in the country. In the United States, the current debate on educational policy is increasingly focusing on the question "whether the state as a monopoly provider of educational services can respond effectively to increasingly rigorous demands placed on the public school system by parents, employers and others" (Plank, 2005). Certain countries have witnessed an intensive public debate on greater diversification of public education (discussed in detail in the next chapter), allowing for different types of schools accommodating different student ability levels or parents' educational preferences.

Common across these countries, with their different traditions, systems and priorities, are the growing demands being made on education as a whole. Education is increasingly in the public eye, which is both recognition of its importance but also a source of pressure for those in the front-lines of responsibility for schooling. There is an increasing awareness in all countries that educational investments lead to significant returns in terms of economic growth and overall societal development. At the same time, the debate on what society gets in return for these financial investments has intensified and has led to growing demands for the accountability of schools.

Attention to evidence regarding perceptions of education, including its priority compared with other sectors making demands on limited public resources, permits discussion of whether the generalised demands placed on education are matched by readiness to support its development. The perception of education as a priority policy sector varies but on the whole it is well up on the public's list. In Japan and most of the Central European countries, education ranks highly compared with other areas of public policy. The reports covering the countries in Central Europe in particular point out that job security and career advancement have become key motives for demanding more extensive schooling. Most school systems have responded by considerably expanding the scope of secondary and vocational education. The Czech Republic among this group of countries providing evidence for this study seems somewhat less positive in measured public support, but even here a majority of the adult population wants to see increased state funding for schooling and higher levels of educational attainment, which are regarded as prerequisites of modernising the country. Survey data from the late 1990s suggested that approximately a quarter of the Czech population was indeed willing to pay higher taxes, provided that those resources are invested in the further development of education.

In Finland, educational institutions are usually ranked towards the top when measuring citizens' confidence in public services. Attitudes differ nevertheless according to social status. Those with vocational education and in blue-collar occupations feel that comprehensive schools function well and criticise reforms as one-sided and hasty. Conversely, those with an academic background and in upper-level white-collar occupations were more likely to criticise the levelling tendency, being altogether more positive about school reforms leading to greater differentiation. Wragg and Jarvis (2003) report that in England education has consistently come second only to health care when survey respondents are asked to choose their top priorities from a list of ten areas. The public level of support for more money for education has, with minor fluctuations, increased over the past two decades. A 2002 survey identified secondary education as the sector most in need of improvement and as the sector of education which should benefit from any additional funding (*ibid.* and Continental Research, 2003). Special education is also singled out as in need of particular support.

The Japanese case interestingly also highlights generational differences in the perception of schooling. According to a "National Survey of Lifestyle Preferences", those born in the 1940s and 1950s assign greater importance to education, whereas those born in the 1960s and 1970s are more satisfied with the current state of schooling. This finding raises the possibility of dissonance between the level of expectation and the level of satisfaction that could lead to disenchantment among the older population.

Parents comprise an important section of the overall population and their views are discussed in more detail below. It is to be expected that they will be most favourable to increasing public support for education as this directly benefits their own children. On the basis of these different findings, however, there is a general level of support for education compared with other potential sources of expenditure, not only among parents. An image of taxpayer "flight" or unwillingness to support education is not the problem it might appear from some political or media coverage: demands are high and the public tends to be a demanding one but this has not significantly dented support. Even where there is through-time evidence, as in England, far from having fallen compared with the mythical "good old days", support for education seems if anything to have risen.

Priorities within education

This study also offers some insights regarding what the priorities within education should be, though parental perceptions specifically are discussed in more detail below. To prepare students for an economy and a labour market increasingly operating on a global scale seems to be a major public concern across all countries. As a consequence, the teaching of foreign languages and ICT skills are increasingly seen as priorities. Both in Finland and in the Czech Republic, people are seriously concerned about the educational system's ability to educate for self-confidence and independence. These kinds of finding serve to balance any blanket assumption that there is a general clamour for more emphasis on the learning and reproduction of factual knowledge as compared with developing understanding and independence. Data in the Finnish Education Barometer, a survey from the latter 1990s about attitudes towards education, shows that opinions about the aims of education differ between rural and urban populations (as do satisfaction levels – see below): urban residents assign greater importance to qualities like the development of self-confidence in students and the preparation for further studies than people living in rural areas.

Recent surveys from England also provide an insight into the priorities for education as seen by the wider population as well as views on how positive change might be brought about. Smaller class size tends to be considered the most effective way of improving both primary and secondary schools (Wragg and Jarvis, 2003). "Better-quality teachers" was the second-most popular measure and others selected by between 10 and 20% respondents were: greater emphasis on developing the child's skills and interests; and more resources for buildings, books and equipment. For secondary schools, more preparation for jobs was selected by 12% of respondents. These findings have remained broadly stable over two decades.

Respondents were fairly evenly divided in their predictions about standards in the future. About a quarter thought standards would be better and 29% that they would be worse (Continental Research, 2003). The five most frequently selected issues on which respondents thought the government should concentrate in order to raise standards in primary and secondary schools were: better discipline/behaviour, reducing class sizes, more teachers, improving the quality of teachers and providing more support for pupils with special needs. The key skills respondents thought that young people should master before leaving school were: English/communications, mathematics/use of numbers, personal development and social skills and ICT. In addition, in answer to an open question "What would it take to make you feel better about education?", the main issues cited were improvements in discipline/authority, resources, funding and standards.

The public's satisfaction with schools – patterns and correlates

Several reports, including those from Finland, Poland and the Slovak Republic, point out that employers are among the most critical about the quality of the education provided in their country. In Finland this is especially clear when employers are asked to grade their education system's ability to meet the changing needs of working life. As direct "receivers" of school graduates they depend to a large extent on the quality and standards of education the system provides and are among the most vocal groups articulating educational demands. More than other sections of society, perhaps, they depend on innovation and change for their professional success and are particularly likely to express demands geared at the content and quality of schools. According to a 2003 report by the Confederation of British Industry (CBI), 34% of employers responding to a survey were not satisfied with the literacy and numeracy skills of school leavers. This broadly fits with the two-thirds of those questioned by Golden (2002) who believed that the quality of local school leavers and of local schools was at least satisfactory. In all countries a significant minority of employers are dissatisfied with the quality of schooling and the range of skills developed in schools, though such criticisms have been a feature of educational commentary since national school systems began.

Across the countries covered in this study, then, those with higher levels of educational attainment are less satisfied with education and they also articulate different demands with regard to the curriculum, laying greater emphasis on personality development and problem-solving skills.

Inhabitants of urban areas express greater dissatisfaction with the current state of education than those living in rural areas, possibly because their proximity to a diversified and demanding labour market makes them more demanding. The lower levels of satisfaction among older people, as for example found in Japan and Finland, might be an important factor as regards the level of political support that schools enjoy in ageing societies and the growing power of older citizens to make their views heard; whether or not this reflects any justified perception of the actual state of education. Women's attitudes towards education tend to be more positive than men's, on the other hand, consistent with the "law" that those who have greater contact with schools and are more involved in schools are more satisfied than those who do not know much about what actually goes on inside them.

Taking these different patterns together, there is not a simple relationship between socio-demographic factors and satisfaction with schooling: both an informed discernment and a proximity to what is going on in education are at play as influential factors and can pull in opposite directions.

Apart from the complexities of the different correlates of satisfaction levels, these findings beg questions about what "satisfaction" means and whether it is an absolute or relative matter. Are the more educated dissatisfied because they believe schools are failing? Or are they more demanding about what schools should achieve and set the bar of success higher? While the pattern of greater dissatisfaction among the more educated is a more or less universal finding, there is no reason to expect the answers to the latter questions to be universal for they will very importantly reflect the actual state of education in different countries which, as underlined by PISA results, still differs widely.

Attitudes, public debate and the media

The media clearly play a significant role in shaping and generating the public perception of education, and the viewpoints of specific stakeholder groups, but specifying more precisely this role is another matter. The media might be used strategically by particular groups wanting to articulate their demands and to make their voices heard. They can also serve as filters articulating certain demands effectively while downplaying others. Some key issues, such as results of international student assessments, failure in schools, student welfare issues and teacher status and salaries, attract media coverage in all countries.

Local and national media play an increasing role in providing parents and other stakeholders with information about the quality of schooling. In some countries, attainment and survey data (including PISA) are widely published and stimulate public debate about the quality of schooling, and in some countries are said to even set the political agenda. In addition to international surveys, some media put together and publish school rankings of their own, geared towards potential customers of education. In this context, the role of the media can be "conservative", because the publication of large-scale evaluation results and attainment data has been used as the basis to argue for returning to "basics".

Research by Hellström and Hellström (2004) about the coverage of education in the Finnish media over the course of 2002 reveals that violence and the maintenance of order and discipline in schools feature most, closely followed by differences in learning outcomes between schools. Even if comparable surveys do not exist for all of the other countries, several background reports point out that negative incidents and findings get more media coverage than school success stories. For England, an earlier study by Baker (1994) concluded that "the middle-market tabloid newspapers in Britain helped to shape a perception of teachers and state schools that is mostly negative and derisory". There are many press reports of employers' views on education, many of which, but not all, are based on anecdotal evidence highlighting negative opinions.

The country reports thus paint a mixed picture about the influence of the media in shaping opinion and demands. On the one hand, increased media coverage of educational issues involves a wider public in schooling and can stimulate necessary public debate about education. On the other hand, negative stories about violence or underachievement can predominate, generating a sense of crisis about the state which schools are now in. From the perspective of education becoming more "demand-sensitive", these are important if unsurprising considerations. Insofar as what people "want" is shaped by jaundiced reporting and little direct evidence, acting on those wants may result in a skewed and negative decision-making process. A question for education systems then is how to make themselves more transparent – an important element of accountability – precisely as a counterweight to perceptions of crisis, when these are not justified by what is going on in schools. Even parents with readier access to what is taking place inside schools can be ambivalent between these messages and their own experiences, between the negative and the positive.

Parental expectations about school education

This chapter examines country evidence directly relating to parental expectations and satisfaction. Demands depend critically on what is expected from schooling. The more that expectations differ from reality the less satisfied will be the key actors, so that satisfaction reflects both perceptions of reality and expectations. If schooling is moving towards more "demand-sensitivity" what do we know about what parents expect school systems to achieve, and how well are these being reflected in provision?

When parents are asked about what it is most important to achieve through schooling, two broad groups of responses – the academic/instrumental and the humanistic – emerge in the answers. In the first, schools should teach children, basic knowledge and skills, leading to good academic results and job opportunities; in the second, schools should cultivate children's humanity and general well-being. How well can schooling meet these expectations of parents, in terms of their internal consistency: does responding to the first cluster necessarily mean neglect of the second or do they reinforce each other? And, how can the system respond to demands and expectations if more is expected of everything – whose expectations should then take primacy and which ones? Again, closer attention to concepts and findings underlines how complex are the elements behind any simple notion of making schools more demand-led.

Divided expectations?

Among the best evidence on what parents expect of schools in the United States (Plank, 2005) comes from a survey conducted by Public Agenda. According to Public Agenda (1994), parents want schools to "put first things first". By overwhelming margins, parents believe that schools should place greater emphasis on providing a safe and orderly environment for student learning, and making sure that children master the academic "basics" of reading, writing, and mathematics. Nearly three-quarters of the respondents identified "too much drugs and violence in schools" as a serious problem, and three out of five identified "not enough emphasis on the basics". This is consistent with the evidence on parents' choices among schools. Parents who have chosen charter schools typically affirm that their choices are based primarily on teacher quality and the quality of the academic programme, and on the school's approach to discipline (*e.g.* Arizona State Board for Charter Schools, 2003; Texas Education Agency, 2003). In this case, the desire for focus on academic results seems unambiguously expressed by parents, and yet the non-cognitive elements regarding behaviour and values are also strong and seen as broadly complementary.

According to a Danish Ministry of Education's survey (2000 and 2003), parents value personal skills and social values even more than academic ones. They consider the five most important skills to be a desire to learn, reading and writing, social skills, confidence in one's own potential, and the ability to make decisions. According to 2003 PISA data, the *folkeskolen* is one of the best educational systems in the world at developing students' desire to learn, co-operation skills and self-confidence. Nevertheless, parents would like to see a greater focus on academic performance and individualised teaching, but not at the cost of "traditional *folkeskolen* values" of which the well-being and a life at ease for the children at school is the core. Danish parents would like to see a more flexible organisation of teaching than they remember from their own schooldays. Greater flexibility in class and group teaching is seen as a means to meet the needs of different learners. Nearly three-quarters of parents want written reports about their child and children's own participation in evaluations is regarded as essential, and exams, tests and marks are given low priority as a means of communication between school and home. A 1997 survey by the Danish Ministry of Education also suggested that all the groups surveyed thought that the requirements made of students were too low: the *folkeskolen* is perceived at being poor at making students accustomed to good working discipline. It is seen as effective in creating an environment in which children thrive but less so at creating enthusiasm and commitment.

Hence even in a system as clearly attached to the humanistic and social aims of schooling as Denmark is, expectations are not straightforwardly about choices between these and more academic ones. In line with the rising expectations about education – a more demanding agenda for schooling related partly to the rising education levels of parents and the public – there is a desire to have all of these more successfully achieved at once. In Japan too, noted for its competitive system and high achievement levels, there seems to be a deal of support for the broader humanistic aims. In a 2002 survey, 5 000 parents in Japan were asked "what they expect of the schools their children attend." Most parents wanted an "education that cultivates humanity and does not overemphasise achievement scores". Asked to what kind of schools they would want to send their children, they responded "schools which train basic skills through a rich natural living experience" (53%); "schools where there is a close partnership between school, home and community and where there are lots of people caring for children", (36%); and "schools catering to different interests and abilities of children" (30%). At the junior high school level, parents wanted schools where students are able to meet different types of teachers and a diversified peer group (36%), schools catering to different interests and abilities of children (32%), and schools having a clear educational philosophy (21%). Items related to a school's potential to develop a student's personality were seen as more important than items related to students' academic achievement.

Parents of elementary school children in Japan have somewhat different expectations from parents of children in junior high schools. "Schools which provide a well-balanced education, with an emphasis upon the acquisition of basic and fundamental skills", are seen as a priority by 28% of parents at the elementary level and 17% at the junior high level. "Schools with high educational standards and quality learning environments, that may educate the talented in global standards", are seen as a priority by 5% at the elementary level and 19% at junior high level. Again, however, the results are complex – such low responses for such apparently important aims of education should perhaps be interpreted in a context where these are adjudged already well achieved.

In the Slovak Republic, parents do not expect schools to prepare for all aspects of life, but they believe that schools should teach an individual to think – providing students with tools through which they can resolve problems. Approximately half of parents feel that the teaching load should be reduced because it is too demanding or too broad, and approximately half of them also think that the content needs to be differentiated better to take individual students' interests into account. Parents expressed significant approval for the development of so-called key competencies in school. Most parents expressed their consent primarily to the support of communication skills and the use of modern information and communication technologies, the ability to resolve problems critically and creatively and to interpersonal and personal skills. The majority of parents favour the use of alternative teaching methods in schools. This does not add up to a narrow "basics" agenda – clearly academic knowledge has its place, but the focus seems to be more on developing higher-order abilities and the capacity in individuals to live autonomously and with others.

The Austrian monitoring survey asked parents and the population (whose responses are broadly similar) about the importance of a variety of different objectives of schooling. Three objectives are rated as very important by about two thirds or more of respondents: vocational preparation, individual autonomy and general knowledge. At the other end of the spectrum, two objectives are rated "very important" by about only a quarter or less of the population – cultural education and factual knowledge. The remaining items are rated "very important" by around 60% of the population: teamwork, social competence, discipline, motivation for lifelong learning, personality development, value education and gender equity, with media competence highly valued by less than half of the population.

The rating of the majority of objectives has not changed much over time. Three have gained increasing support – personality development, general knowledge and value education – while two have lost ground (individual autonomy and factual knowledge). With regards to the question about what schools should see as their primary responsibility and what should be seen as less important, again parents' responses do not differ much from those of the wider population. Schools are seen as responsible for vocational preparation and for general knowledge. Parents are seen as responsible particularly for discipline, individual autonomy and value education, and somewhat less for personality development and social competencies. This is not a simple picture; parents do not expect schools to do everything, and yet most things are judged to be important, there is no simple dichotomy between academic and humanistic goals.

In Poland, research suggested changes took place in parents' ambitions for their children after the political and economic transformation (CBOS, 1996). Parents have been above all determined to protect their children against the negative effects of the economic transformation, particularly unemployment, but also against other forms of social exclusion, for example an inadequate ability to use computers. A study conducted four years later shows that the majority of Polish parents would like their child to get a university education, both daughters (73%) and sons (69%) (OBOP, 2000). In England, too, evidence of the importance attached to good academic results is provided by the common expectation amongst parents that their children will remain in education beyond the statutory leaving age. Batterham (2003), for example, reported that the vast majority of London secondary parents expected their child to stay on in education and training beyond the age of 16. Three-quarters expected their child to go on to higher education. This was most strongly expressed by minority ethnic groups. Parents with a university degree or higher qualification were more confident that their child would go on to higher education (91% compared with 74% for the sample as a whole).

A Hungarian survey on parents' expectations of schooling showed variation in parents' expectations by school type and social position. Parents of lower-level secondary school and vocational training school students in Hungary find the development of competencies and skills most important, but the satisfaction level is only average. The higher the mother's school attainment, the more emphasis is given to the development of problem-solving skills. Less educated parents rather perceive schools as places where information is transferred. Parents living in urban areas assign greater importance to helping students to become highly educated while, as we see below, perceiving schools more negatively than parents in rural areas. More than half of parents living in urban areas in Hungary think that students have to learn too much information instead of learning how different things are connected. More than two-fifths of parents feel that they cannot give the necessary help in learning to their children – a strong correlation with school attainment. Especially parents living in Budapest and the more educated are of the opinion that the school does not teach students to learn.

In Hungary, parents' main expectations are: "developing students' competencies and skills", "preparing students for the next level of schooling" and "teaching students to learn and developing their problem-solving skills". Of these, parents are most satisfied with their children's preparation for the next level of schooling, while they are clearly dissatisfied with the development of problem-solving skills. Transferring information was ranked the highest concerning satisfaction but among priorities it was ranked on the middle of the scale. Parents are also satisfied with education for honesty and morality, which was ranked last but one on the list of importance. Preparation for the next level of schooling is ranked first among parents' expectations and they are relatively satisfied with it. The expectations that got the least overall support ("providing peaceful and caring learning environment", "developing students' life skills", "educating students to become honest adults with high moral standards") – were ranked first or among the first by a sizeable minority of parents – 20 to 25% in all. There are thus some interesting signs of dissonance between what is judged important and how well they are felt to be achieved. This is in some contrast with Finland as shown by 2000 Nordic School Barometer. Most people agree that instruction in their native language, English and mathematics are important subjects and that social and natural sciences are also important. Asked how schools are succeeding in providing instruction in these different subject areas, Finns feel that schools are largely successful.

In sum, there are some differences between countries, but it is not possible to conclude that there is either any simple division between countries or between parents on what they think is important. That said, areas of education which parents judge to be consistently modestly or poorly achieved, despite their assessment of their importance, can provide very useful indicators about how well school systems are performing. There is a subtle underlying relationship between objective conditions and subjective assessments – the Polish example of shifting support towards the instrumental "survival" ends of education in rapidly-changing conditions is a good illustration. What also comes out of the results is a sense of stability of both aims and ratings which, were the system to be genuinely "demand-led", might add up to a rather conservative agenda for schools. The groups which might be expected to be the drivers of change – the middle classes being wooed by politicians – are also those who have tended to do best with the system as it is. The issues of equity are explored further in the discussion of satisfaction next. It is not clear how far the orientations to the demands of the "clients" of schooling (if this means the parents), however refreshing the contrast with "supply-led" may sound, adds up to an agenda of reform.

Parental satisfaction with schooling

Are parents satisfied with schools in view of what they regard as their key aims? What do parents think about the schools their children attend and what do they think about the state of education in general? Are some sections of the parental population particularly positive or disgruntled? The English evidence on these questions is among the most detailed of the country reports. Here, parents of school-aged children tend to be more positive about standards in schools and education than the general public. Eighty-two per cent of parents of primary school children rate the standard of primary education as "good" or "very good" compared with 60% of all adults (Continental Research, 2003). Similar differences are found regarding standards in secondary schools albeit based on somewhat less positive assessments: 69% of parents rated standards as "good" or "very good" compared with 41% of all adults. Parents' views on some aspects of education, however, tend to be less positive than those of teachers (Continental research, 2004): only just over a third of parents agree that primary school standards has improved over the last few years compared with 45% of teachers who think so. Whereas 42% of parents thought their children were "very well" taught, 81% of teachers and governors opted for "very well" taught.

Data from Spain (Ombudsman, 2003) show that the majority of parents in Spain express a high level of satisfaction with their children's schools and again with significantly higher levels of satisfaction with primary schools than with secondary ones. A survey conducted in 2000 (Danish Ministry of Education) indicated three-quarters of parents as satisfied with their children's schools. The Danish report notes a paradox between the high levels of user satisfaction on the one hand and the widespread criticism of *folkeskolen* in the public debate on the other hand: the satisfaction survey from 2002 showed that 78% of parents were satisfied or very satisfied with schools in Denmark. According to a University of Turku study (2001), seven out of ten Finnish parents were fairly or very satisfied with the standard of instruction provided by schools. Just over a quarter of all respondents gave a very positive feedback about their children's school, while about one in seven respondents were dissatisfied. Parents seem to be more critical in Poland, as in "Do Polish Schools meet their Goals?" (2001), there are almost an equal number of parents satisfied and dissatisfied with the Polish educational system – 43% and 42% respectively.

Nevertheless, the common finding in the countries included in this study is for parents to be relatively positive, and more positive about schools than the general public, of which they are only a section. US and English evidence is in line with a related finding which has been noted in many countries: that parents tend to be more satisfied with the schools that their own children attend than with schools in general. In the United States, parents consistently rate their own children's schools higher than schools in general. These findings may be related to parents' sources of information about schools. According to Public Agenda (1997), nearly three out of four parents rely on "personal observations and conversations" for information about their local schools, while three out of five rely on the media for information about schools outside their own community. Parents who choose their children's schools are consistently more satisfied than those who enrol their children in the schools the state chooses for them (*e.g.* Texas Education Agency, 2003; Arizona State Board for Charter Schools, 2003).

Batterham (2003) found that among secondary school parents in London 51% were very satisfied with their own schools compared with 16% with London schools in general. This may be because London parents tend to exercise deliberate choice of schools more than elsewhere in the country – they both feel the need and are able to do so – or it may be another example of gloom regarding the general state of affairs despite personal experience. There is not everywhere, however, findings consistent with the pattern of (greater) "distance from school" (negatively) influences attitudes about schools. In Austrian education surveys, no marked differences are reported in most questions between the assessment by parents and the assessment by the general public. Some Czech research findings even go against the "distance" thesis: a 1997 survey showed that just over half of general public respondents expressed satisfaction with the quality of schooling but the proportion of satisfied parents was smaller (45%). Teachers, far from being favourable, formed the most critical group, with less than a third (31%) happy with the state of education (Goulliová and Průšová 1997). Perhaps they feel most affected by reforms or such factors as low salaries, though it is interesting that such dissatisfaction does not find an echo in the assessments of parents of the students under the charge of those teachers.

The country reports also provide some insights on those aspects which parents feel are achieved more or less well at different levels of the educational system (primary, secondary and other). The majority of parents of children going to secondary schools in London thought that the schools their children attended were delivering well on the range of subjects taught, the quality of school management, teaching, security and resources. In general English secondary schools are considered by parents to be more in need of improvement than other phases of education: about half consider it needs improvement compared with only about a fifth who judge this for primary education (Continental research, 2003). The parents' main reported priorities for improvement were: reduction in class size (selected by over 50%); more teachers in schools (selected by over a third); and a greater focus on literacy and numeracy (selected by more than 25%). Other priorities were: more support staff help; improving the quality of teachers; support for students with special needs; a curriculum relevant to the 21st century; and support for "failing" schools.

A survey conducted in 2000 (Danish Ministry of Education) showed parents in Denmark are most satisfied with their communication with teachers, teachers' proficiency and attention to individual children. Parents would like to see better cohesion between day-care centres, schools and recreational arrangements, more opportunities for parental involvement, more attention given to the abilities and needs of individual children and better books and teaching material. An earlier parental survey in Denmark (Danish Ministry of Education, 1997) showed that there is a widespread perception that *folkeskolen* are better suited to younger students than to older ones. With regard to teaching students fundamental skills, parents of children at these schools feel that this is done well, although they want schools to focus more on fundamental reading and arithmetical skills. Parents in Finland are more satisfied with teaching and assessment and less about catering to the needs of individual children. According to a University of Turku study in Finland (2001), instruction was considered to be better at lower secondary level compared with primary level, not worse.

In the Slovak Republic, in six crucial areas of schooling – overall level of the school, level of training and care of children, quality of teaching, individual approach to children, quality of information on students' attainment and personal development of children – the most positive evaluation went to the kindergartens, then secondary grammar schools, then primary schools and last vocational schools. The compulsory primary school was ranked one before last in three evaluated areas (in overall level, level of training and school's care of children and in the quality of informing parents about students' learning results). In all types of schools, the personality development of children received the worst ratings.

Countries vary widely in how they see schools to be dealing with the challenges they are facing. Among the Czech parents surveyed for the 2003 PISA study 37% expressed total satisfaction with the school attended by their child and another 54% of parents said they were fairly satisfied. Czech parents believe that the school maintains discipline well and do not see any socio-pathological disorders in the children (drugs, alcohol, and violence). However, while parents are generally satisfied with the operation of schools, almost one third of the respondents believe that schools fail to make full use of their students' potential and that there is a lot of room for improvement. Asked how the Austrian education and training system cope with important challenges – equal opportunities for both sexes, integration of disabled students, integration of migrants, support for gifted students, support for less able students, information about drugs, coping with difficult students, reduction of the volume of the syllabus – about half positively rated the way schools are coping with these challenges. The assessment of coping with challenges is less favourable than the overall satisfaction with schools. In the United States, nearly three-quarters of the respondents identified "too much drugs and violence in schools" as a serious problem (Plank, 2005, see next section). Shaw (2004) reported that about half the English parents in that study think that bullying is a problem and nearly half consider truancy to be problematic. Hence, even generally positive parental assessments do not translate into a perception that all is equally well achieved.

Some of the country studies refer to trends. In England (Continental research 2004), only just over a third of parents agree that primary school standards has improved over the last few years though 45% of teachers think so. In Japan, according to a 1995 survey of 3 600 presidents of Parent-Teacher-Associations (National Congress of Parents and Teachers Associations of Japan, 1995), some two-thirds of those surveyed answered that they were "satisfied" or "very satisfied" with Japanese schools. But while in 1979, 27.5% of those surveyed said that they were "very satisfied" with primary education, only 21% were in 1995. For junior high schools, this high satisfaction rate dropped from 26% in 1979 to 16% in 1995.

In some contrast in Hungary, most believe that today's children are expected to work much more than students of their generation were and three-fifths of parents say that schools prepare students for further studies better than schools did when they went to school. This opinion is held especially by the less educated, older parents and those living in smaller settlements, while less than 50% of parents living in the capital and those with higher education agree. This might reflect either the objectively lower provision for the rural population and those with lower attainment in earlier times, or the more demanding expectations among the better-educated and urban population. Whereas overall, two-thirds of parents in Hungary said they were more or less satisfied with teaching, this also was lower among the more educated parents, older ones and those living in Budapest. The next section focuses on these social patterns.

Parental attitudes to schooling are not as negative as often portrayed in the media. The overall satisfaction of parents with education systems is high throughout all countries, even if there are noticeable regional and gender differences with regard to the perception of educational quality. In most countries, parents of school-age children tend to be more positive about the quality of schooling than the general public. Women are more likely to perceive themselves as being involved in their children's schooling than men, and research in several countries indicates that women/mothers express greater satisfaction with the content and quality of education than men/fathers do. The parents involved in schools are more positive than those who are not. All this suggests a relationship between "distance" from schools and the levels of (dis)satisfaction about schooling. Those who do not have much day-to-day interaction with schools and teachers can develop stereotypical images of schooling. They rely on the media images described at the beginning of this chapter which tend to be negative. Those who meet school leaders and teachers, especially if they interact and collaborate with them, are better able to appreciate the work the school is doing. Even parents who report negatively about the general state of schooling can be much more positive about the local school.

Issues related to equity – background of parents and different types of schools

The Polish country report describes how parental opinions on how schools meet educational goals are related to their level of education: the better educated the parents, the more likely they are to express a negative opinion. The most critical are parents living in larger cities who hold high expectations that schools will start their children on a professional career. However, parents from small towns and villages are also critical when it comes to ensuring a high level of knowledge and equal standards for students from different social groups. A great majority (72%) of the polled parents from towns with fewer than 20 000 inhabitants believe that schools do not provide for equal chances for better life (CBOS, 2001). This might reflect a growing disparity between the perceived quality of educational provision in urban areas and in the countryside. While in cities availability of choice between different schools provides exit options and enhances the quality of schooling, the inhabitants of rural areas are constrained by the limited number of schools available to them.

Spanish families, whose children are schooled together with less than 10% of children with a distinct ethnic origin, tend to be more satisfied (64%) than those families whose children are in a school with more than 30% immigrant children (Ombudsman, 2003). Only 48% of them consider the school to be good or very good. A different pattern emerges in the case of immigrant families. They express a high level of satisfaction with those schools which their children attend, independent of this factor. This might indicate that satisfaction with the education of younger children is higher, possibly because labour market demands for "employability" do not impact on parents' judgement of schooling at this early age.

According to a University of Turku study (2001), seven out of ten parents were fairly or very satisfied with the standard of instruction provided by schools. In terms of the effects of background variables, the most considerable differences appeared to be in line with educational background and occupational status. The most positive attitudes towards the Finnish education system were held by those with vocational education. Attitudes became steadily more critical among respondents with higher levels of education. On the other hand, respondents with an academic background and in upper level white-collar occupations are more satisfied with the fairness of schools than those with vocational education and in blue-collar occupations, despite the latter's reluctance to seek reform.

Hence, there is thus a complex – contradictory? – set of attitudes which is by no means specific to Finland. Those with lower levels of attainment will often judge that a system which is serving others well has not fairly dealt with them and yet have higher recorded satisfaction levels. Those with higher attainment are satisfied with their advantaged access to educational benefits and do not wish to see that threatened, but their lower satisfaction suggests that they wish that what they (or their children) have access to could be even better.

A Danish parental survey showed that older parents were more positive than younger ones; it also mirrored the findings elsewhere in reporting the lowest level of satisfaction with *folkeskolen* was found in the Copenhagen area, whether reflecting objective or subjective differences. As regards types of school, parents of children at *folkeskolen* who also had experience of private schools were less positive in their assessment of the former than parents whose children had only been to the first. Parents whose children attend private schools tend to be more satisfied (more than half very satisfied) than parents of children at *folkeskolen* (only 20%), and almost a quarter of them had considered moving their child to a private school during the previous year. Parents of children at private schools are, in particular, more satisfied with the adaptation of teaching to the abilities and needs of individual students, academic requirements, social atmosphere in the classroom and class size (Danish Ministry of Education, 1997).

In the Slovak Republic, the country report refers to as many as four-fifths of parents agreeing that the state should run primary schools. Ten per cent of parents, mainly private entrepreneurs and parents with only one child, express a preference for private primary schools. Relatively few parents supported church-run primary schools. Three-quarters of parents agree with state secondary schools, though nearly half of them believe that the parent should have the right to choose the best school for their children. One-third of parents – especially men, parents from cities, parents with university education, private entrepreneurs and parents with a single child – supported the development of private secondary schools, with a higher proportion (40%) of parents against the development of private schools.

In Poland, among parents of students at the newly-created *gimnazja*, more than half were glad that their child attends a *gimnazjum* rather than a lower-level secondary school and a quarter was disappointed because of that (Konarzewski, 2001). Few parents see the *gimnazjum* as a place for separating good students from weaker ones but rather as a place which can help their child achieve a high level of education (Konarzewski, 2001, p. 143). On the whole, parents' opinions on how schools meet educational and social goals are more positive in the case of the non-public, namely civic and private schools in Poland (Putkiewicz, Wilkomirska and Zielinska, 1997). The perceived advantages of non-public schools are seen to be the smaller class sizes, a focus on developing students' individual interests, and innovative curricula and methods of teaching as fostered by young teachers.

This section has drawn attention to the complex nature of the relationships that are involved as regards satisfaction and its relation to expectations. We have noted the strong relationship between knowing what is going on inside education – "proximity" as described here – and positive appreciation of what is achieved. But we have also seen that this cuts across two other "laws" or tendencies. First, is that the urban middle classes are the least satisfied, which in turn may reflect the difficulties faced by schools in urban areas or else be a more subjective generality about setting benchmarks higher. Second, those who have most gained from schooling – precisely the educated parents and their children – are most likely to believe that it is fair.

General discussion

This study is based on different national case studies in their turn based on datasets particular for their countries. In practice this means that there are problems in comparing the results and that there are many blank spots because countries do not collect systematic evidence on attitudes, expectations, or satisfaction, whether of parents, employers or the public at large. This review has shown the value of exploring this area and of making the evidence base more robust. If education systems wish to be both more "demand-led" and more "evidence-based", this is a terrain where there is much work to do in terms of data collection and of developing mechanisms for feeding the results into the broader debate and decision-making process.

This chapter has brought together a body of, albeit rather sketchy, evidence relating to both the public's and parents' attitudes towards schooling. Should improved evidence relate to everyone in order to clarify the general patterns and findings? How far to focus on particular sections of the population, such as those who gain least from education at present, for instance, or employers? Do parents and the public deserve an equal voice?

This is not so much a data collection issue as one about who should be listened to if schooling is to be more "demand-led". In the context of this chapter, this concerns how attitudinal data should be used to inform decision-making.

The most obvious argument can be made for it to be parents, on the grounds that it is their children at school – they have the greatest stake in ensuring the "best outcomes" as the school's "clients". But as this chapter has shown, parents will naturally be most concerned about those outcomes relating to their own children, which may or may not coincide with the best interests of children as a whole, still less society as a whole. We have seen that privileged parents – whose voices tend to count most in the political process – are more likely to perceive the educational system as fair, in part precisely because it has served them relatively well and may oppose reforms designed primarily to serve others. Theirs may be a conservative agenda, in a literal sense of the term. And, of course, it is not at all clear that schooling should be viewed as an area of social life which is about responding to "clients", a market metaphor which is anathema to many.

If not of parents, then whose demands? There are many candidates. It might be those who pay – the taxpayer. It might be those with a particular stake in the competencies and values of who emerges from schooling, including the higher education sector and employers. It might be a more general notion of the public and of society. And, of course, there are the learners themselves, as discussed in Chapter 5. The case can be made for all of these, and no doubt others. At one extreme, the problem in the face of such diverse "demands" is that being "demand-led" may be no more than a smokescreen for defending the status quo: responding to parents, children, employers and the public at large is what all education systems already claim to be striving towards. Hence without much clearer notions of what "demand-led" means, and whose demands should be listened to, this direction for reform risks being an empty slogan. At another extreme, seeking to respond to diverse demands, schools may be pulled in many different directions at the same time. This will make it difficult to schools to devise coherent strategies.

What about the evidence itself and what it reveals about attitudes towards schooling? First, there are some general messages. There is a stronger belief in the value and achievements of schooling than many might expect. In many places, education is a higher public priority than other calls on the public purse. Even where satisfaction is lower – in part because objectively the quality of provision is cause for concern – belief in education's value tends to be high. This should reassure many working in education who may often feel beleaguered but it can also contain an anti-reform message ("if it ain't broke, don't fix it"). Those responsible for education need to weigh up the implications of these essentially positive judgements.

There is another general message to be underlined. There may be some differences of emphasis, but people want more of everything that is good: in other words, they are very "demanding" about education. Within the lack of clear message that is the high (and possibly rising) expectations about schooling is another which is more pointed: neither parents nor the public have simplistic agendas that can be summarised either with terms like "basics" or with their opposite about making young people "happy". In fact, the different publics when asked have complex, demanding agendas not slogans. Dealing with the different demands will cause tensions, for the system and for individual schools.

Second, there are differences to be highlighted. What comes through clearly from the available data on satisfaction is that the closer people are to schooling provision or the education system, the more satisfied they tend to be about it. This "rule" is manifest in different ways: parents with children going to school are on average more satisfied with schooling than other parents and the public; parents who are involved in school governance are more satisfied than other parents; women (who tend to participate more in school life) are on average more satisfied than men; the younger are more positive than older adults. Again, the message is generally positive, as knowledge of or experience with education leads to higher levels of satisfaction. However, the long-term legitimacy of schooling and the willingness to pay taxes to support it rest on the satisfaction of all. Increasing accountability and transparency of school systems may actually serve to "spread the word" about the achievements which are most obvious to those closest to what takes place in schools and classrooms.

There are other differences related to satisfaction highlighted by this chapter. First, parents in urban areas tend to be less satisfied with schooling than parents in rural areas. An issue for policy is to ascertain how far this is a reflection of the difficulties faced by schools in urban areas or instead whether there are more demanding standards set by urban parents. What also comes through in the review is that the more educated tend to be less satisfied than the less educated parents. There might well be some overlap between these two patterns, as those with higher attainment levels tend to congregate in urban and suburban areas. Such differences may serve, in a demand-led system, to exacerbate inequities – an issue to be addressed in the following chapter on choice and diversity. As regards parental perceptions and equity, it will be especially important to make sense of the apparent contradiction between educated parents saying that they are less satisfied but believing the system is fair as against the less educated expressing satisfaction with what is on offer but with a greater sense of exclusion from the benefits.

References

Andersen Møller, A. *et al.* (2001), *Forventninger og færdigheder – danske unge i en international sammenligning* (Expectations and skills – Danish young people in an international comparison), AKF, DPU and SFI-Survey.

Arizona State Board for Charter Schools (2003), *Findings from the 2002 Survey of Parents with Children in Charter Schools: How Parents Grade Their Charter Schools*.

Baker, M. (1994), "Media Coverage of Education", *British Journal of Educational Studies*, 42, 3, pp. 286-297.

Batterham, J. (2003), *London Challenge: First Survey of London Parents' Attitudes to London Secondary Schools* (Research Report 493), DfES, London.

CBI (2003), *Employment Trends Survey 2003*, CBI, London.

CBOS (1996), *Aspiracje edukacyjne Polaków. Ocena wykształcenia narodu i kosztów edukacyjnych. Komunikat z badań* (Educational aspirations of the Poles. The level of education of the nation and the costs of education – assessment. Report from research).

CBOS (2001), *Czy polskie szkoły wywiązują się ze swoich zadań?* (Do Polish schools meet their goals?).

CBOS (2002), *Do czego przygotowują absolwentów polskie szkoły średnie?* (What do Polish upper secondary schools prepare their graduates for?).

Continental research (2003), Department for Education and Skills Stakeholder Tracking Study. Waves 1-3 (COI Ref. 250473), available: *www.dfes.gov.uk/research/project*

Continental research (2004), Department for Education and Skills Stakeholder Tracking Study 2003 (Waves 4-6). Summary Report (COI Ref. 257682).

Danish Ministry of Education (1997), *Forventningsundersøgelse – folkeskolen i søgelyset* (Survey of expectations – focus on *folkeskolen*).

Eder, F. (1998), *Schule und Demokratie*, Studienverlag, Innsbruck.

Golden, S. (2002), *Report on Employers and Training Providers in Phase 3 EIC Partnerships*, Report 17/2002, NFER, Slough, United Kingdom.

Goulliová, K. and P. Průšová (1997), *Veřejnost a školství '96* ("public and schooling '96"), čitelské noviny.

Hellström, M. and R. Hellström (2004), "Koulupuhe mediassa vuonna 2002", *Luokanopettaja-lehti* 1/2004 ["School talk in the media in 2002", *Class Teacher Journal* 1/2004 (in Finnish)].

IEA (2003), PIRLS 2001, "International Report: IEA's Study of Reading Literacy Achievement in Primary Schools".

Konarzewski, K. (2001), *Drugi rok reformy strukturalnej systemu oświaty: fakty i opinie* (The second year of the structural reform: facts and opinions), ISP.

Koulutusbarometri (1995), Helsinki: Opetushallitus ja Suomen Gallup Oy (Education Barometer 1995. Helsinki: National Board of Education and Suomen Gallup Oy).

Koulutusbarometri (1996), Helsinki: Opetushallitus ja Suomen Gallup Oy (Education Barometer 1996. Helsinki: National Board of Education and Suomen Gallup Oy).

Koulutusbarometri (1997), Helsinki: Opetushallitus ja Suomen Gallup Oy (Education Barometer 1997. Helsinki: National Board of Education and Suomen Gallup Oy).

Koulutusbarometri (2000), Helsinki: Opetushallitus ja Suomen Gallup Oy. (Education Barometer 2000. Helsinki: National Board of Education and Suomen Gallup Oy).

Ladd, H.F. (2003), "Introduction", in D.N. Plank and G. Sykes (eds.), *Choosing Choice: School Choice in International Perspective*, Teachers College.

Mäntysaari-Hetekorpi, H. (1996), *Vanhemmat ja peruskoulu – tutkimus koulu- ja koulutettavuustulkinnoista. Joensuun yliopisto* (Parents and the comprehensive school system – a study into representations of school and educability. University of Joensuu. In Finnish).

Matějů, P. and J. Straková, J. (2003) (eds.), *Vyšší vzdělání jen pro elitu?* (Upper education only for elite?), ISEA, Prague.

Ministry of Education, Warsaw (2001), *Społeczny obraz reformy, Edukacja 1997-2001. Raport* (The social view of the reform. Education 1997-2001. Report).

National Congress of Parents and Teachers Associations of Japan (1995), *The Realities of PTA's and Parental Opinions on Education*.

NHK (2002), Public Polls, Japan.

Nordisk Skolbarometer (2001), Attityder till skolan år 2000 (Attitudes towards schools in 2000) TemaNord, Nordic Council of Ministers, Copenhagen, p. 547.

OBOP (2000), *Opinie o reformie oświaty w lutym 2000 roku* (Opinions about the educational reform expressed in February 2000).

OECD (1995), *Public Expectations of the Final Stage of Compulsory Education*, OECD, Paris.

OECD (1997), *Parents as Partners in Schooling*, OECD, Paris.

OECD (2003), *Student Engagement at School: A Sense of Belonging and Participation, Results from PISA 2000*, OECD, Paris.

Ombudsman (2003), *Informe: La escolarización del alumnado de origen inmigrante en España: análisis descriptivo y estudio empírico*, Vols. I & II, Madrid.

Public Agenda (1994), *First Things First: What Americans Expect from the Public Schools.*

Public Agenda (1997), *Good News, Bad News: What People Really Think About the Education Press.*

Putkiewicz, E., A. Wiłkomirska and A. Zielińska (1997), *Szkoły społeczne i szkoły państwowe. Dwa światy socjalizacji* (Civic schools and state schools. Two models of socialization), Społeczne Towarzystwo Oświatowe.

Shaw, M. (2004), "It's Getting so Much Better all the Time", *Times Educational Supplement*, 10 September.

Taylor, Nelson and Sofres (2003), *Public Perception of Education, Summary Report*, TNS, London.

Texas Education Agency (2003), "Texas Open-Enrollment Charter Schools: Sixth-Year Evaluation".

Turku University (2001), *Turkulainen koulu elämänuran muokkaajana, meneillään oleva tutkimushanke. Turun yliopisto* (How does a school in Turku influence career development? An ongoing research project. In Finnish).

Williams, B., J. Williams and A. Ullman (2002), *Parental Involvement in Education* (Research Report 332), DfES, London.

Wragg, T. and L. Jarvis (2003), "Pass or Fail? Perceptions of Education", in A. Park, J. Curtice *et al.* (eds.), *British Social Attitudes: The 20th Report – Continuity and Change over Two Decades*, Sage, London.

Chapter 3
PARENTAL CHOICE AND DIVERSITY OF PROVISION

This chapter shows how choice is an increasingly important mechanism for parental demand. Countries are moving towards greater parental freedom to making choices with better information available to make their decisions. There are also significant moves to widen the diversity of programmes and schools among which choices can be made, including through private provision and, in some countries, home schooling. The evidence does not permit any comprehensive evaluation of different choice mechanisms but it does show that individuals and groups are not responding in the same way. The better educated, middle class parents tend to exercise their choice options more frequently. There are differences between urban and rural areas, partly a reflection of the social profile in these areas and partly because of the greater number and range of schools in towns and suburbia.

In recent years in the countries covered here, the basic model of a school within the district of residence and close to the family home, sometimes with an elite private system co-existing alongside, has been modified. This chapter outlines the range of change that has taken place along the dual axes of promoting diversity and establishing room for the exercise of parental choice. In the change which has taken place on both axes, parental demand has clearly been an important factor, whether at the broad level of political demand from influential stakeholder groups (including educated parents) which governments have been keen to satisfy or at the local level with parental behaviour influencing provision on the ground.

The concept of demand enters in more than one way. Enhancing the range of options can be regarded as a means for schooling better to respond to different demands – individual and collective – with parents, families and community interests seen as the "clients" of education. We have also seen in the previous chapter that those who have actually exercised choices, such as through taking their child from the neighbourhood public school to attend another, often have higher measured levels of satisfaction. The exercise of choice among similarly-organised schools of different profile or among different types of school altogether is an example of "exit" behaviour – to return to the Hirschman (1970) distinction that has informed our analysis – in that accessing a chosen different school, or even abandoning formal schooling altogether, means to leave another school behind. The consequences of different choice structures and decisions need to be examined empirically. We can be clear nevertheless that this report is not premised on the assumption that maximising choice is a universal policy objective; and the attention given to enhancing demand should not be equated with a commitment to maximise choice.

Schooling policies and the room for choice

This section reviews features of the current situation regarding parental choice of school. The issue of parental choice policies has long been controversial. Critics insist that policies to promote it imply acceptance that some students will enjoy a better education than others, that market principles have found their way inappropriately into the public enterprise of schooling, and that the cohesion of a shared national project has been abandoned. Advocates regard it as a route to higher quality through the injection of a modicum of competition, and the healthy reflection of the principles of sensitivity to demand and diversity into the uniformity of education systems. In the countries reviewed, choice options have been widened though this is a much more central element of the policies of some than others.

Denmark illustrates well the different arguments. Policies on school choice have triggered a public debate. Free choice exercised by the better educated and better off may be to the detriment of the rest, an effect which is seen at odds with Danish ideas about equity. In Denmark, parents have had the right to enrol their children in a municipal school other than the district school if the school was willing to take the children. Now, the municipal council may decide to let parents choose freely, within the guidelines set out by the municipal council, between district schools and other schools in the municipality. More than 75% of Danish municipalities offer a choice between the district school and other schools in the municipality. The proportion is highest among the large municipalities. The number of rejections of students who apply to transfer to a school other than their district school is very limited. Approximately 9% of students want to go to a school other than the district school and 86% of these requests are granted. The majority of rejections is because the municipality has decided on a class-size limit that they do not wish to exceed by transferring further students (Danish Ministry of the Interior and Health, 2004). Recently, the room for choice has been further extended to allow freedom of choice across municipal borders which will be given a trial period of two school years.

In Finland, students may apply to a school other than the one assigned to them, which may admit them at the discretion of the education provider. Currently, the majority of students in basic education are admitted to their local school. When selecting students for a non-assigned school, all applicants must be subject to equal selection criteria. If a school has developed a special profile, it may use tests to determine students' aptitudes and other selection criteria have included the presence of siblings, students' language choices, and the school's curricular emphases. Nevertheless, the local authority may decide that children living within its area should be given priority in education that it provides. Clearly, in a sparsely populated country like Finland, the distribution of choice is very uneven: in small municipalities, which may only have one comprehensive school, there is little choice; in the major cities, there are plenty of options.

A fairly conventional and stable situation exists in Austria. Each child belongs to a certain school district and if parents want their children to attend another establishment, this is also possible if a place in the school of choice is available. There are, however, considerable regional differences influencing the opportunities for school choice. At the lower secondary level, the academic track is available mostly in urban areas. At the upper secondary level, the supply is concentrated to cities. Some types of special schools are available only in one or very few localities. Access to primary education is basically regulated on a local matching model which gives each child access to a particular school. However, there is room for choice of another school if parents find a school that accepts the child. Choice thus depends on the supply of accessible schools which is related to population density and opportunity for mobility. Transport costs are covered by public funds.

In Hungary, pre-schools and primary schools are not allowed to hold entrance exams, and the school of the parent's choice is obliged to enrol any child of compulsory education age living in the district. To those living outside their district, admission may only be denied due to lack of places. Due to the decrease in the number of children, lower secondary schools in Hungary have free capacities to develop special profiles responding to demand in recent years. The Hungarian data suggest that there is a clear-cut correlation between social class and expectations and behaviour with regard to making decisions about schooling. In households where the head of the household has only the lower-level secondary school qualification, 90% of children attend the district school, while this ratio is 73% in the case of parents with university or college qualification. Better educated parents in many cases choose a school for reasons other than it being closest to their home.

When the state monopoly on education was eliminated in 1990 in Poland, the supply of education diversified: individuals, organisations and churches were given the opportunity to establish schools. Instead of mandatory enrolment of a child at the nearest school, the reforms gave parents the freedom to choose a school for their children. Legally, parents are free to choose any school, but in reality choice is limited. Tuition fees charged by non-public schools and admission procedures deter certain families from choosing these schools. Parents choosing civic schools (see below) do so because they believe they offer better relations between the teachers and students, more individualised teaching and learning, smaller classes, and richer educational opportunities.

In the Spanish Constitution parents are given the right to choose the appropriate education for their children. Autonomous Communities apply criteria in the selection of students when demand outstrips the supply of places. Apart from criteria such as the proximity to the family home or simultaneous attendance of siblings at a particular school, *centros concertados* (publicly-funded private schools), use the previous attendance of children in the non-compulsory pre-school within the same school as a criterion and are thereby shifting the main pressure of demand down from the first compulsory grade (at age 6) to the first pre-school grade (at age 3). In Spain, the criterion most mentioned by parents for choosing a school is the proximity to their home, given by nearly half of both Spanish (42%) and immigrant families (47%). The quality of school preparation is the second criterion (29% and 20%, respectively). But then, the item "diversity of students" as a positive reason for choice is seen differently by Spanish (only 3%) and immigrant families (13%).

In England, parents have the right to say which school they would prefer their child to attend, regardless of the school's location, but there is no guarantee of a place at the school if there are more children wanting to attend that school than there are places available. Nationally, nearly three-quarters of parents applied for a place in their nearest state school. Parents in metropolitan areas are often able to choose from a range of local schools and London parents are less likely to apply to their local school (some 60 000 children attend schools outside their home Local Educational Authority's [LEA] area). The admissions authority follows a set of rules to decide who should be offered a place, which authorities may use different criteria in different areas. If the child is not offered a place at the parents' preferred school, they have the right to appeal to an independent panel and if this is upheld, the admission authority is under a duty to admit the child to the school. Out of the approximately 70 000 appeals lodged in England against non-admission to a secondary school in 2002/2003, about one-third were decided in the parents' favour. According to Flatley, Connolly and Higgins (2001) over 80% of parents were offered a place in the school they most wanted, and not surprisingly, the large majority of parents were satisfied with the selection process. However, in London, fewer than 70% of parents were offered a place in the school they most wanted.

The most common reason parents gave for choosing a school was good academic outcomes at around 40% of parents, and conversely the most frequently-cited reasons given for not selecting the nearest school were poor discipline, rumours of bullying and poor academic results. Batterham (2003) found that the six top reasons of London parents for sending a child to a school in a different LEA were: the school was higher in the performance tables than those in their area; religious ethos; the good reputation of other schools; the school was easier to travel to than schools in their home area; the poor reputation of the schools in their home LEA; and their child's happiness. In England, the groups most likely to cite academic reasons for choosing a school were those living in London, non-white ethnic groups, owner-occupiers, and families with mothers in higher occupational classes. Groups least likely to do so were: those living in rural areas, those renting in the social sector, white ethnic groups, and families where the mother had never worked.

Promoting diversity

Promoting diversity is a natural accompaniment to promoting choice: if provision is perceived to be broadly similar there is no need to expect parents to be clamouring to change from one school to another. The English government has in recent years pursued a policy of diversifying supply. A 2002 Act requires the local authority (LEA) to announce where a new secondary school is required. Then any interested party can put forward proposals for a new school: a community or religious group, an LEA or another public, private or voluntary body can publish proposals, which are judged on the basis of their educational merits, value for money and the outcome of consultation. At the same time, English state schools have been given considerable freedom to specialise and to offer additional benefits and services. Specialist schools place particular focus on their chosen subject area while meeting the National Curriculum requirements. Any state school in England can apply to be designated as a specialist school in one (or two) of ten areas: arts, business and enterprise, engineering, humanities, language, mathematics and computing, music, science, sport and technology. City Technology Colleges (CTCs) are independent non-fee-paying schools for students aged 11 through 18 that offer students in urban areas the opportunity to prepare for gainful employment. They also offer a wide range of vocational qualifications post-16 – alongside those qualifying for university entry. Academies are publicly funded all-ability independent schools that attempt to provide a first-class free education for local students.

There are approximately 7 000 schools with religious affiliation in England within the state education system of which the large majority (about 6 400) are at primary level. The vast majority of those 7 000 schools are Church of England (4 700) or Roman Catholic (2 100). The other religious groups represented – Jewish, Muslim, Sikh, Greek Orthodox, and Seventh Day Adventists – make up the other 3%. All faith schools are required to teach the national curriculum and for religious education, they may opt either to teach their own faith or to follow locally agreed religious education syllabuses.

In Hungary, schools organise the education and teaching of their students according to their own school curriculum based on the National Core Curriculum. Many general and secondary schools offer an advanced programme in one or more subjects, most often in a foreign language, mathematics, science, physical education and music. Some offer subjects that are not taught at other schools (*e.g.* history of art, drama, spatial informatics). Some general secondary and specialist schools (*e.g.* dual-language or artistic vocational schools) organise entrance examinations, but the majority of secondary schools do not. The Ministry has now ruled that only those institutions with at least twice as many applicants as places may do so. The majority of schools now rank students by their educational performance at the previous school and admit them based on this ranking. This performance ranking has a strong correlation to the school attainment of parents and makes the system very selective. Well-qualified parents in particular are ready to send their children to another school if the one their children attend does not meet their expectations. Alternative schools are financed by local government and of these the Steiner network is the most extensive, with a few Freinet, Montessori and Rogers schools as well. There are dual language schools where some or all subjects are taught in a foreign language. Church schools are increasingly under pressure to admit students from any background; Catholic schools, however, usually ask for credentials concerning the belief of the parents while other denominations are more permissive.

Czech legislation provides for the establishment of schools and classes with a specific focus that provide extended teaching in foreign languages, physical education, mathematics and natural sciences, music, visual arts or information technologies. Ten per cent of all students attend these schools. Parents show great interest in extended teaching in languages and sports and demand is around twice as high as the number of places available. In the

Slovak Republic, centrally managed schools, as in communist times, proved unable to respond to the new requirements of society and the labour market. Recent governments have therefore pursued a gradual decentralisation of the system, with greater autonomy given to individual establishments. At primary level, parents are now able to choose from a range of schools including those with alternative philosophies such as Steiner and Montessori. It has now become the aim of policy makers to increase the supply for education through a range of opportunities allowing for individual choices to be made.

Secondary general schools in Poland have considerable freedom in developing their curriculum and differentiate salary schemes resulting in different levels of quality. Some educational programmes which go beyond the basic curriculum standards can only be provided in richer communities and in urban areas. Strong competition and school rankings as popularised by the media help to maintain a high quality of education in these cases and the gap between urban and provincial schools is thus widening. Students are admitted in line with the decision of the school director, which is taken on the basis of the results of the entrance examination, results of previous education and other evidence of capability. Most parents exercising their right to choose schools scoring well in public rankings are from the highest socio-economic status, leading to a growing concern about a social selection of students. *Gimnazja* are willing to enrol outstanding students from outside their own area and sometimes even put them into separate classes offering better educational conditions.

Curriculum choice among options

Another source of choice and diversity, which is not about choosing between schools, is through options within schools themselves. In Finland, choices are most commonly made in relation to language studies. Elective additional courses may also be selected in mathematics, physics, chemistry, biology and geography. The majority of those studying the first three of these subjects are boys, whereas the gender distribution for the last two, biology and geography, is fairly well balanced. Conversely, optional languages are more commonly chosen by girls than boys. In England, students have some degree of choice over the subjects they study at key stage 4 (age 14-16). In Japan, senior high schools can offer various subjects and courses, and students may select the school and the course from academic to vocational courses, or select various programmes in the newly introduced comprehensive departments. The school curriculum at the compulsory education level is by and large standardised across the country, but at junior high school level, students may choose additional subjects in accordance with their career choices, interests or special ability. This system of optional subjects is not yet fully driven by the diversity of "demand".

A more demand-driven system is currently considered for the post-compulsory education level in Japan. The Central Council for Education advocated a diversification of curricula in its reports of 1996 and 1997 ("The Model for Japanese Education in the Perspective of the 21st Century"). The Council stated the necessity of paying special attention to children with learning difficulties and of further developing more individualised forms of education responding to individuals' abilities and aptitudes. At the high school stage, programmes called "Super-Science High School" and "Super-English Language High School" have been developed to improve "opportunities for the talented and well-motivated students in specific fields".

The Slovak education system developed from the position of a unified school system prior to the revolution to the current diversified, democratic and humanist school system. The system of training and education responds to the fact that each student is a unique personality. It gives the student the possibility to choose one course from a group of subjects, according to his/her interest besides the compulsory curricula subjects. In the lower grades, the possibility of selection is more modest, however, while in the higher grades it more fully suits the requirements of students. In Poland, students of institutions of compulsory education have no influence on the choice of teaching programmes and textbooks, though they are sometimes able to choose additional afternoon classes.

Diversity as a consequence of collective demands

This chapter discusses choice and diversity; however, there is strong connection to voice. It is often specific and strongly-voiced demands of collectives that generate diversity in the education systems. In most countries, demand is expressed most strongly for educational services not yet or not sufficiently offered by the state. It is expressed to make policy makers aware of gaps in the public provision of education. Examples of this would be the demand for pre-school education and after-school programmes. Improved nursery and kindergarten education has been widely discussed, for example, in connection with the improving of the employment situation of women. Moreover, several reports single out demands coming from parents asking for faith-based instruction as do the parents of children with special needs.

Ethnic and linguistic demands

Ethnic and linguistic diversity has for a long time been a social reality in many OECD countries. Most countries seek to accommodate the needs of their diverse student population in some form and this section describes some of these rights and opportunities. However, these also raise some of the most fundamental and controversial questions arising in schooling today. What is schooling for? Where should the balance be struck between system-wide integration of all populations and basic uniformity, or else the recognition, even nurturing, of difference? In particular, what role should the formal public school system play? The recognition of diversity and competing claims raises particular questions for enhancing sensitivity to parental demands. Several reports mention the strength and frequency of demands made by parents asking for faith-based instruction (as they do for parents of disabled children).

In Finland, the Swedish minority, which represents about 6% of the population, has the right to education in their own mother tongue. Similarly, members of the Sami population, an indigenous community, are guaranteed the right to maintain and develop their own language and culture. Students speaking the Sami language must primarily be provided with basic education in that language, should their parents so choose. In Finland, the language of instruction at an institution providing general upper secondary education is either Finnish or Swedish. Other possible languages of instruction are Sami, Roma or sign language, and it is also possible to provide instruction primarily or entirely in other foreign languages as part of a separate teaching group or institution. In the matriculation examination, a foreign-language student may, instead of participating in the mother tongue test intended for Finnish-, Swedish-speaking or Sami-speaking students, take a test in Finnish or Swedish as a second language.

Children of an age for compulsory schooling who have entered Finland either as refugees or asylum seekers may receive preparatory instruction in their own group for six months before they start comprehensive school. At comprehensive school, these children, like other immigrant students, are usually put into classes appropriate for their age and skills. There is a special appropriation for providing immigrant students with the opportunity to receive special remedial instruction and instruction in their mother tongue. The objective of immigrant education is to prepare immigrants for integration into the Finnish education system and society and to support their cultural identity, so that, in addition to Finnish or Swedish, they will also have a command of their own native language.

The Slovak Constitution guarantees the members of national minorities a right to education in their native language, namely Hungarian and

Ukrainian. In Hungary, the diversity of supply is increased by national minority pre-schools and schools in which education is provided in the languages of the seven fairly small national minority groups (Greek, Croatian, German, Romanian, Serb, Slovak, Slovenia). In these educational institutions, the language of the particular national minority is taught as a foreign language to those whose first language is different. The same holds true for the Polish minority education in the Czech Republic. In Poland, the visible renaissance of national and ethnic identity has led to the foundation of separate schools or classes for children from national minorities. Members of national minorities have the right to education in their national language. Larger minorities with the appropriate number of students can form a class or school of their own. In view of the fact that other minorities are dispersed throughout the country and the number of students is small, their right to education is exercised in the form of complementary programmes subsidised by the state. Members of the German minority enjoy support in the form of extended teaching of German at lower-level secondary schools and the establishment of bilingual lower-level secondary schools.

In the Central European countries, the education of Roma children and children of migrating parents remains a very serious challenge. In Poland, special classes have been established to prepare Roma children before they enter lower-level secondary school. In the Czech Republic they attend special classes before entering a primary school. The schooling of Roma children, whose educational attainment is far behind the national average, has become a policy priority in Hungary. Whether this is because of increasing demand expressed by Roma special interest groups, or because society perceives Roma education to be inadequate deserves further exploration. The fact that education is not provided in the Roma language due to the lack of parents' demand, might indicate that the new interest in Roma general education is actually driven by those other than the Roma themselves. The Hungarian government tries to prevent a segregated education of Roma children and legitimates the Roma schools only if they are established or supported by the Roma minority self-governments.

In the United States (Plank, 2005), increasing opportunities for school choice and other policies that facilitate exit from the traditional state-centred education system have created space for the articulation and accommodation of a variety of heterogeneous demands. The most important of these are efforts to institutionalise educational opportunities responsive to, and supportive of, the cultural and religious preferences of particular groups. Among charter schools, for example, diversity manifests itself primarily on the dimensions of ethnicity and language, and not on the dimensions of curriculum and instructional strategy (Fuller, 2003). Many parents who school their children at home have chosen this option in order to protect cultural and religious values that they feel are not sufficiently honoured in the traditional public school system.

Religious education

There is no uniform policy trend across countries with regard to the provision of religious education in schools. Some countries have made provisions for students to be educated in their respective religion/denomination, whereas others pursue a secular line by keeping religious education separate from public education. Even in those countries where religious education based on a particular faith is offered, parents (and students above a certain age) are allowed to decide whether they want to take part in the lessons or alternatively take religiously neutral classes in "ethics".

The overwhelming majority of Polish inhabitants are Catholic, and the norms and values of the Catholic Church are thus perceived as "general norms". Religious education has become a permanent element in the Polish school curriculum. The Catholic religious education curriculum is defined by the "Catechetic Directorate of Catholic Church in Poland" (2001), a document supplementing Vatican instructions. Initially this was welcomed, because formerly religion could only be taught outside the education system. However, the dominant place of Catholic religious instruction in the school curriculum soon came to be criticised by liberal circles. A 1999 law enables parents to decide whether their child should attend religious education classes or ethics classes. The importance of religious schools, most of them Catholic, among non-public schools has grown since 1990 – in the school year 1999/2000 they accounted for 23% of non-public primary schools, 35% of *gimnazjum* and 47% of upper secondary schools of general education.

Students in all schools in Finland have the right to religious instruction in accordance with their own denomination. About 85% of comprehensive school students participate in Lutheran religious instruction and students who are not members of that Church may choose between religious instruction and ethics, a multi-disciplinary subject that includes elements of philosophy, social sciences and cultural sciences. When parents of at least three students demand non-Lutheran religious instruction at a school, it must be provided. In upper secondary schools, students themselves can demand it. The National Core Curricula determine the contents and objectives of religious instruction in accordance with the beliefs of the respective church. The curricula for other religions are drawn up in accordance with general objectives set for religions within the National Core Curricula. In the Czech Republic religious education is taught as a voluntary subject in those schools where parents of at least seven students express their request to have this class opened. There is a debate now about the establishment of ethics as a mandatory and religiously neutral subject.

The diversity of religious (and non-religious) student backgrounds poses important questions with regard to educational demand. Should schools respond to demands for instruction in specific religious beliefs? Should they respond to religiously motivated demands concerning the content of school curricula? Or should schools, in principle, act as counterweights to religion, offering a secular "citizenship education" for all? Given the number of immigrants from different religious backgrounds, few countries are spared these tough questions, made more acute by the growing presence of religious fundamentalism which is not restricted to any single tradition or faith. Far from the religious factor quietly disappearing from the educational policy agenda as secularisation grows – which assumption underpinned thinking in many countries in the latter half of the 20th century – it is a very prominent issue with no obvious sign of disappearing in the 21st century.

Demands for recognition of special needs

Several countries report that parents of disabled students have been very vocal in demanding change. In the past, disabled children have often been catered for by separate schools, a situation that parents frequently perceived as leading to the isolation and marginalisation of their disabled children. Many countries have responded to the requests of those parents and parent associations by making provisions for disabled children to be integrated into mainstream schooling.

In Austria and the Czech Republic, for instance, based on the wishes of parents of disabled children, new regulations for integration into school have been amended step by step in the last decade. There are regulations which give additional resources for integrated classes. Basically, there is now a right for disabled children to be educated in the mainstream of primary and lower secondary schools. Parents have to apply, going through a formal procedure. Schools have also a say in the decision whether they want to set up the preconditions for integration, mainly providing a second teacher for integrative classes. In Hungary, kindergarten-level children with special educational needs are usually integrated, whereas there are segregated special schools by types of disability or special classes in regular schools at the primary and secondary level. Similar to the Austrian policy, at parents' request, however, there are opportunities for disabled students to participate in integrated education. In the Czech Republic, parents can request an integrated education for their disabled child, but the child needs to pass through an assessment procedure and the school must be able to offer an appropriate infrastructure. In England, the great majority of disabled students are educated in ordinary schools.

Parents with special needs, then, tend to be very articulate in expressing their demands to the educational system. This opens up a range of interesting questions for the overall notion of demand. It would be interesting to do further research on the question whether other special interest groups, whose children potentially suffer from discrimination in the educational system, have been as articulate in expressing their specific demands and have been similarly successful in achieving certain aims. Have the parents of recent migrants, for example, wished and been able to express demands for special language tuition? Such examples can build up a picture of the power of "voice" to widen "choice" and the ability of specific groups to "work the system" in pursuit of their wishes.

Diversity through alternative forms of schooling

This section examines diversity in more marked forms – not diversity of programmes or emphasis within a shared structural model but through different models: selective and non-selective schools, public and private schools, and formal schooling and home schooling. Several countries have moved to greater diversification of public education, allowing for different types of schools accommodating different student ability levels or parents' educational preferences. The role of demand is clearly a central element in their emergence and differing fortunes. This in turn is closely, but not exclusively, related to the familiar factors of social advantage and reproduction as well as to critical issues of value choices and beliefs. The two are not unrelated and parents may choose, say, publicly-funded private schools of religious denomination to gain social advantage for their children as well for reasons of belief, apart from any more neutral perception of educational quality.

Selective and non-selective schools

Those countries with a selective school system – in this study, Hungary, Austria, Poland, the Czech Republic and to some extent England – report that privileged parents tend to send their children to them. These parents expect that, owing to strong selection, their children will be learning among better-motivated students with a similar background, among which serious behaviour problems and drug abuse are less frequent. In the Czech Republic, admission to *gymnázia* (selective schools leading to university education), is based on selection consisting of written and oral examinations, and sometimes intelligence tests. The school intake is determined by the school administration and ranges from 6 to 14% of the relevant age group, depending on the region, with the number of applicants double the intake number. *Gymnázia* were re-established in 1990 and aim to provide a more demanding, academic form of education. They are predominantly supported by parents with a high level of education and social status, and often seen as unjust by parents with lower-level educational degrees. The Czech School Inspectorate concluded that the segregation of more talented students has resulted in a gradual decrease in the standards of lower-level secondary schools. There is thus much debate on the issue, and the new education bill approved in 2004 stipulates only one national curriculum for both types of lower secondary education, an equal number of teaching periods and an identical level of pay of teachers. However, the selective admission procedures for *gymnázia*, which penalises children with lower cultural capital, have been preserved.

Research conducted in Hungary has also shown the familiar correlation in the distribution of students between schools of different standards and the school attainment of parents (Andor and Liskó, 2000). Students attending general secondary schools account for nearly 80% of children of parents with a university qualification, falling to 60% of children of parents with a college qualification, 40% of children of parents with a secondary school-leaving certificate and only 20% of children of parents with a vocational training qualification. Neither conservative nor liberal governments have abolished the six- or eight-grade general secondary schools due to the explicit demand of the most powerful parents' stakeholder groups. In Poland, civic schools which select students based on results of entrance tests are dominated by children of white-collar workers and businessmen. Research by Zawadska (1992) showed that parents from Warsaw were more positive towards civic schools than parents from smaller cities. As many as one third of respondents in rural areas claimed that the creation of private schools was a negative phenomenon, though at the same time the majority of respondents considered such schools to be better than state ones. This might well reflect a sense of growing inequality by the inhabitants of rural areas where civic schools are not as readily available as elsewhere.

In England, the majority of schools do not select on ability. A 1998 government act ruled out any new selection by ability, except for post-16 education and banding arrangements. Existing grammar schools and schools that already had selective admission arrangements were allowed to continue with those arrangements. In a survey by Taylor, Nelson and Sofres (2003), the public was asked to say whether "children should go to a different kind of secondary school according to how well they do at primary school" or whether "all children should go to the same kind of secondary school no matter how well or badly they do at primary school." Opinion was evenly divided on this issue in 2002, with 49% selecting each option. However, the population share supporting non-selective schools increased from 40% in 1984 to 49% in 2002 whereas the proportion endorsing selective education remained the same with fewer "undecided". Parents' views on selection are similarly divided. According to an earlier MORI survey cited by Lambert (2002), 52% of parents believed independent school standards were higher than those in the state sector, and 68% believed that there was a role for the independent sector in the UK educational system. This study also found that 53% of parents would choose an independent school for their child if they could afford it, stating higher standards as their reason.

The role and perception of "private" schooling

Schooling tends to be primarily a public service, as shown in Figure 3.1. There is more variation the higher up the system one goes from primary to lower secondary to upper secondary. Even though public education, publicly financed, remains the dominant model, there are a number of countries where there are significant departures from this even at primary level – especially in the Netherlands and Belgium. The purely private provision is also discussed later in this chapter. Though numbers of students may not be high in most countries, its social role and importance can far outweigh any simple balance of numbers (as in the United Kingdom). The figure does not suggest that there is yet a major departure from the core model in OECD countries. But it does usefully illustrate that there is already a degree of variation. And, as this chapter shows, the trend is for the range of choice and diversity to be getting wider.

Even if private schools are limited in most OECD countries, most school systems offer parents the choice between public and private schools, and this is revealing of the extent to which education is regarded as a "good" that people should be able to buy and how far alternatives to public provision are tolerated, even funded by the state. Countries pursue different policies on this issue: in some, private education is fully or partly funded by the state, in others it is fully paid by parents. The extent to which parents opt for private rather than public education can also be interpreted as a strong indicator of "exit" behaviour, depending on how far it represents a genuine cost to the household (not just another publicly-funded alternative). The school systems covered in this report are all predominantly public, but most countries make provisions for the establishment of schools based on private initiative.

Especially in the Central European countries (Hungary, Poland, the Czech Republic and the Slovak Republic), private education has been defined as a political and civil right and is seen as one means of contributing to a pluralistic society in the post-Soviet era. The creation of a large number of alternative schools in the Central European countries has been largely parent-driven and is a sign of an increasing readiness to express specific "demand" in the domain of education. Many, in some systems the great majority of, private schools are operated by religious denominations, while attendance in them does not necessarily indicate a religious commitment of parents. It is often motivated by the demand for a quality education set in a normative pedagogical framework: private schools are often selected because of their smaller class size, a focus on developing individual interests and sometimes their innovative curriculum and methods. Most systems have created a legal framework in which reformist schools can be founded and to a certain extent financially supported. In Spain and Finland, for example, private schools are financed by the state and are not allowed to charge fees. Private schools in England and Poland, on the contrary, are largely financed through fees.

Figure 3.1. Distribution of enrolled students, by type of institution (2003)

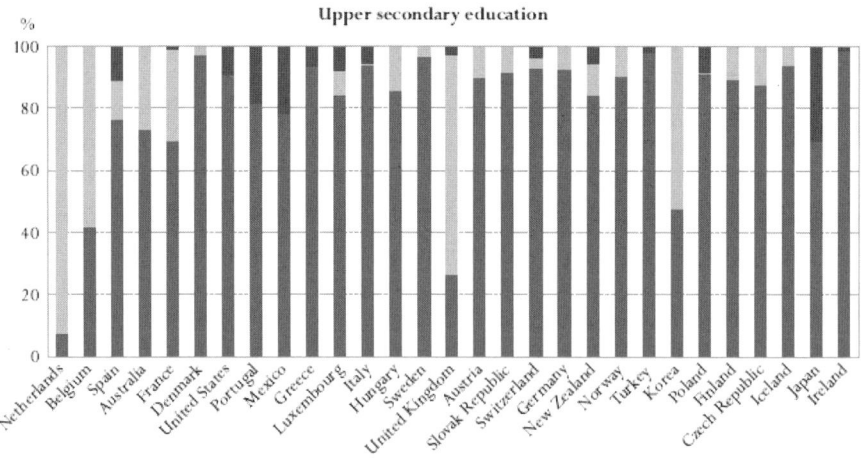

Note: Countries are ranked in descending order of the percentage of students enrolled in the private institutions in primary education.

Source: *Education at a Glance: OECD Indicators 2005*, OECD, Paris, Table D5.1.

Japan is an example of a country where the number of students enrolled at private schools is extremely small at the compulsory education stage. In addition to conventional public schools, which are publicly maintained and managed, the Ministry of Education has admitted schools established by public authorities and managed by private companies or bodies. For now, it is limited to kindergartens and senior high schools and excludes other schools of compulsory education. Schools with a religious affiliation are always private in Japan. State schools are not supposed to provide any religious education because of the principle of secularism and the separation of church and state laid down in the Japanese constitution. Currently only 0.9% of all elementary schools in Japan are private, according to the Ministry's 2003 School Basic Survey Report.

The Scandinavian tradition is also one of a very strong public sector, but the numbers in private schools are certainly higher than in the Japanese case and tend to be growing. In Denmark, the number of students at private independent primary and lower secondary schools is relatively stable with showing a slight, continuous increase. These schools must meet the standards of what is generally required at *folkeskolen* and there is a requirement for a minimum number of students. These private schools define their own basic principles and evaluate their teaching themselves. They are managed by a board of governors with a majority of private individuals. The schools are supervised by parents and by an additional person chosen by the parents to supervise whether the school's overall teaching meets the *folkeskolen* standards. The schools are granted an operating subsidy paid out according to the number of students per annum, calculated on the basis of the corresponding public expenses at *folkeskolen*, less the parents' fees (that are comparatively low, currently under one-fifth of public subsidies). Private independent schools in Denmark are diverse: urban schools with a focus on traditional academic and cultural values, specialised boarding schools, religious or church schools, small schools based on progressive ideas, schools with a specific educational objective like Steiner schools, immigrant schools or German minority schools.

Education in Finland is free of charge for students and private schools are not allowed to collect student fees. The majority of private schools in Finland are publicly funded and under public supervision. They follow the national core curricula and the requirements of the competence-based qualifications confirmed by the National Board of Education. In order to receive the same amount of public funding as municipal schools, they have to apply for a licence at the Ministry of Education. As part of granting a licence to provide basic education, the government may also assign a specific task to the provider. Such a task has been assigned, for example, to Steiner schools, religious schools and foreign-language schools. Even if the licence is not granted, the private school concerned may still be established, but it will remain outside public supervision and will not receive public funding. There are very few private schools. Currently, only about 1% of schools providing basic education are private, and students at these schools account for 2% of all students in basic education.

The national authorities in Hungary pay a *per capita* grant for each student which covers about 60 to 80% of the costs of providing an education. The remainder is covered by whoever runs the school, most often the municipal government in the case of public schools. Private schools try to raise the remainder from parents' contributions and the donations of other supporters. The financing of church-run schools is different because since 1997 all denominational schools in Hungary have received the amount that covered the costs of a child's schooling the year before. Currently, 90% of the younger children (aged 3 through 14) attend a government or municipal pre-school or lower-level secondary school financed from the central budget. In secondary education, the percentage of students at private schools is considerably higher than at the primary level with a sixth of general secondary school students at church schools. This high percentage does not necessarily indicate the religious commitment of the parents but often the demand for a quality education.

Private schools in Poland can be divided into: i) fully private schools, owned by individuals or private entities; ii) civic schools, founded and owned by civic organisations; and iii) religious schools run by the Catholic Church, orders and other religious organisations. Most private primary and secondary schools are civic schools, established by organisations of parents and teachers, and these function as non-profit organisations. In this regard, they are thus distinct from the *centros concertados* in Spain. The subsidy allocated to those schools now covers 100% of expenses incurred per student. They are known for their extra-curricular activities and their innovative curricula. The schools in the private sector proper, on the other hand, tend to be exclusive establishments with high monthly fees enabling the schools to offer a rich curriculum and comfortable classrooms in order to meet parents' expectations of returns for their private investment. In the 2003/2004 school year, private sector units ran 4% of all primary schools, attended by 1.3% of all primary school students; 8.3% of all *gimnazja*, attended by 1.8% of the total *gimnazja* students; and 19% of post-primary schools and post-*gimnazjum* secondary schools, attended by 4.1% of those students. Private schools were mostly created by the highly-educated, among those many self-employed entrepreneurs.

A debate about educational equality started with the creation of the first private schools in Poland in 1998. Some people saw the main aim of schools to be in reducing educational inequality and demanded that all schools be open to all students. Others tolerated inequality and accepted private schools financed mostly by parents, at the same time calling for lower taxes for those who pay for their children's education themselves (Putkiewicz, Wilkomirska and Zielinska 1997). The difference between the two sides of the debate is reflected in the two types of non-public schools – civic and private. Civic schools stake their claims in the needs of the local society with the co-operation of parents, teachers and students while private schools stress their professionalism in offering educational services to students and parents treated as "clients".

The overall proportion of pupils in private schools in Austria is about 7% and this has increased slightly in recent years. About two-thirds of all private schools are run by religious organisations: 90% by the Catholic Church (under public regulation, according to agreements with the Vatican), 5% Protestant, and the rest by others. Except for a very few elite establishments and some alternative schools there are no marked differences between private and public schools nor a strong distinction between these systems, because the private sector is mainly under public regulation, and the largest group among them, the Catholic schools, receive public funding for teacher salaries. Different rules for public subsidies apply for different kinds of private schools. Most private schools, except for the Catholic ones, charge high fees. Private schools are more strongly represented in Vienna and are equally divided between the compulsory and post-compulsory cycles. Over the last few decades, other types of free or alternative private schools have also developed that follow their own pedagogical models. To get official credentials, students from those types of private schools have to pass external examinations. However, the numbers of those free schools are quite small (less than 50 schools with less than 1 000 children in total).

In Spain, too, there is far less of a distinction between public and many privately-run schools because of the high level of public subsidies to the latter. In this case, however, the number of students and schools is much higher than in Austria. There are three different types of schools: public, private, and private schools with public funding, the *centros concertados*. Public schools are basically financed by the Autonomous Communities, and partially funded by the City Councils; they represent approximately 63% of the total of the compulsory-level schools. All Spanish nationals have the freedom to create and direct private schools except under exceptional circumstances (a criminal record, etc.). Parents and teachers are by law involved in the control and management of all schools receiving public funds, namely public schools and *centros concertados,* through the school council, each one of which develops its own "educational project" on the basis of the common core curriculum.

In England, private schools – including the so-called "Public Schools" – are not funded by the state and obtain most of their financing through fees paid by parents and income from investment. All independent schools, both day and boarding, must be registered with the central authorities (the Department for Education and Skills) and must reach and maintain standards set out in specific regulations covering the quality of education provided, the spiritual, moral, social and cultural development of students, the suitability of proprietors and staff, the premises and accommodation, the provision of information for parents, and the way in which complaints are dealt with. Those standards are inspected either by the Office of Standards in Education (Ofsted) or by the Independent Schools Inspectorate every six years. In January 2004, the majority of students (91%) went to state schools, about 7% attended independent schools and 1% attended maintained and non-maintained special schools. The share of students aged 16 or over in private schools is comparatively high since students in independent schools are more likely to remain in education beyond the statutory leaving age.

Home schooling

Another, more extreme dimension of "exit" is through choice of home schooling, where this is permitted. Opting out altogether of the education system provided by the state is a form of rejection of available public supply. Tolerance, even encouragement, of home schooling also reflects the extent to which a society considers education to be a public or a private matter. The largest number of students schooled at home live in the United States, where home schooling is a legal right in all 50 states. The other end of this spectrum in the countries covered is Japan, which has a strong "obligation of attending schools" and does not permit home schooling. Twenty-eight states in the United States require home-schooled children to undergo some kind of official evaluation, either by taking standardised test or submitting a portfolio of their work. Thirteen states simply require parents to inform officials that they are going to teach their children at home. According to the *Economist* (2004), the US Home School Legal Defence Association claims that as many as 2 million students are currently schooled at home in the United States. A 1999 survey by the Department of Education put the number at 850 500 students. It is unclear from such figures how far the traditional "home school family", coming from religious groups who reject institutionalised education, remains the typical profile.

Whatever the actual numbers involved, home schooling is not of equal interest in the European countries participating in the study; in these, it is still a marginal phenomenon involving mostly children who are seriously ill, disabled or exceptionally gifted, as well as some who fit the religious profile outlined above. In Denmark, children must be taught but they do not have to attend a school. Parents may teach children at home, ensuring that they receive an education on a par with that required at *folkeskolen*, but this is in fact very limited. In Finland, there is no obligation to attend a school and the compulsory period of education may also be completed by studying at home. In such cases, the municipality of residence is obliged to verify a child's progress in his/her studies. As in Denmark the number of those studying at home is very small. Similarly, it is "education" that is compulsory in England, not schooling *per se*. About 1.5% of children of school age in the United Kingdom are currently educated at home (Lambert, 2002). Parents are not required to follow the National Curriculum or to keep school hours; they do not need to be teachers or to hold any other special qualifications. If a child has never attended a school, the parents do not need to take any action prior to starting home education. If the child has already been in school, the parent must formally deregister the child by writing to the principal. Local education authorities must ensure that parents are providing suitable education for their child.

In the Central and European countries, the number of students schooled at home is also very small. What is of particular interest in these cases is the key role of the school and its principal in the decision-making process, rather than an authority or inspectorate further removed from local provision. In Poland, home schooling is still a marginal phenomenon, but interest in it has been growing steadily. Parents who want to exercise this right must obtain the permission from the principal of a public school within the boundaries in which the child lives, who also specifies the requirements that must be met and the way of checking the child's development. In Hungary, compulsory education may be achieved through home schooling. The school principal, the authorities and the child welfare services must examine whether the parent's choice is in the interest of the children. Students schooled at home are obliged to take exams in compulsory subjects. If children with special educational needs, learning difficulties or behaviour problems are home schooled, teachers prepare them for exams while those schooled at home at their parents' request must rely on their parents for examination preparation. New legislation permits home schooling at the primary level based on a request from the parents to the director of the school where the student has been admitted. Principals may grant permission to a student with special learning needs or unusual talents to proceed according to an individual education plan. The student's parents or guardians must show serious reasons for this form of individual education and ensure appropriate conditions for learning at home. The home educator must have completed secondary education.

A controversy about the abuse of home schooling was triggered in 2001, when there were several complaints which alleged that parents of children seen as problematic were persuaded to home school their children. It was alleged that in some cases parents were threatened that unless they did so their children would be expelled from the school. Since then, the Ministry of Education has supplemented the law to prevent schools from using the option of home schooling as a means of discriminating against Roma students.

General discussion

Chapter 1 proposed that demand-led schooling implies a different role for voice and a greater role for choice. The countries covered in this study show indeed that they are moving towards greater choice: greater parental freedom to choose, a more diverse supply, and better information about the supply for parents to base their choice on. In almost all countries, parents are increasingly entitled to choose the school they consider most appropriate for their children. Most often this takes the form of allowing parents to send children to a school outside their own school district. The information available to parents has improved as well. Policies have sought to make the public sector more transparent by increasing public accountability. For schools this may mean that their academic results or profiles are available to the public. Demographic factors are playing their part: with fewer children born, and funding often based on student numbers, schools are increasingly competing for students instead of selecting them.

All this is in line with the position of the earlier OECD/CERI choice review (Hirsch, 2002) which observed that the notion of "choice" has had a real if varied impact on education systems, and that a situation in which many families exercise an active choice over which school a child should attend, rather than taking it for granted that it will be the local one, has become a permanent feature of education systems. It also suggested that in parallel with policies to allow more choice of school, education systems have moved away from a model in which such decisions are taken solely by those who deliver the system – the professionals and administrators. This trend may be recast in the terms of this report – that such change may be seen as about making education systems more "demand driven". The question we may still ask is: "yes, how far?'.

This chapter has also examined a critical aspect of choice through the diversity in what is offer. There are the choices and diversity of programmes within a shared structural model. But more fundamentally perhaps, there is the diversity that comes through the creation or encouragement of different models: selective and non-selective schools, public and private schools, and even the choice of home schooling in preference to formal education. Arguably, these forms of choice opportunities are likely to have an even more profound impact than giving parents greater freedoms to choose between putatively similar schools.

Several countries have moved to greater diversification of public education, allowing for different types of schools accommodating different student ability levels or parents' educational preferences. Most systems offer parents the choice between public and private provision albeit with different understandings about what these terms cover: in some, private education is fully or partly funded by the state, in others it is fully paid by parents. Most countries make provisions for the establishment of schools based on private initiative, including in recognition of value choices and beliefs. Opportunities for choice between different schools, within the public system and between public and private provision, have become the rule rather than the exception. Even the Nordic countries, where belief in schooling for public good and equity is as strong as anywhere, have seen significant reforms in this regard. This has been to recognise, even encourage, the use of "exit" strategies as well as shift the balance between public and private behaviour in shaping education systems.

It is meaningless in an educational context to be "in favour of" or "against" choice in general – it all depends what these choices are, who is able to exercise them and what the impact of one set of choices is on the opportunities of others. Even so, it is clear that analogies with demand from private markets have definite limits. Parents in free education systems do not express demand by their willingness to pay a particular price for the service, and there are limits on how much they want to switch between "products" in response to quality judgements given the disruption it would cause for their children.

The equity concerns about increasing choice are familiar and well-rehearsed. This report does not permit any kind of systematic assessment of different choice arrangements against equity criteria. But, it does confirm that better educated, middle class parents are more likely to avail themselves of choice opportunities and send their children to the "best" school they can find. Reinforcing cycles can become vicious circles: with a higher intake of better-performing students the performance of the school will go up, improving further the status of the school; for the other schools the cycle works in the opposite direction with the danger of an increasing gap between highly-performing and under-performing schools. There are also clear differences between urban and rural areas, in part for the simple reason of the greater number of schools to choose from in urban areas. Public policy must take into account these possible consequences when redesigning educational systems.

The chapter has raised other concerns which go beyond judgements about the social equity of different choice options. They relate back to the distinction made in Chapter 1 between individual and collective voices in demand. How far should particular community demands be met through the school system? This simple question raises some of the most controversial issues arising in schooling today. How far is the school about system-wide integration of all populations and nation-building, part from any specific academic ambitions? Or else should it be the crucible for the recognition, even cultivation, of difference? When does healthy multi-culturalism stop and the promotion of anti-social, inward-looking particularism begin? Is school *par excellence* a secular institution or a legitimate place for the expression of religious beliefs? More generally, what is education for and within that the specific role of the formal public school? Enhancing sensitivity to parental demands takes us straight into these fundamental questions. They do not sit easily with an essentially technocratic view of policy, which assumes that issues can be decided by reference to an evidence base.

We can also ask how "choice" relates to "voice" as discussed in the next chapter. If parental choice of schools is encouraged, parents might look for alternatives and eventually take their children out of a school instead of changing or improving it. On the other hand, providing options for choice can be a response to demand and may provide powerful incentives for development, both in those schools and classes being chosen and in those rejected. These are important political and educational questions, and it is as yet unclear how far they are about trade-offs or instead mutually compatible ends.

References

Andor, M. and I. Liskó (2000), *Iskolaválasztás és mobilitás*, Iskolakultúra, Budapest, Hungary.

Bagley, C., P.A. Woods and R. Glatter (2001), "Rejecting Schools: Towards a Fuller Understanding of the Process of Parental Choice", *School Leadership and Management*, Vol. 21, 3, pp. 309-325.

Batterham, J. (2003), *London Challenge: First Survey of London Parents' Attitudes to London Secondary Schools* (Research Report 493), DfES, London.

Danish Ministry of the Interior and Health (2004), Structural Commission, *Undervisningsministeriets sektoranalyse af folkeskoleområdet* (The Danish Ministry of Education's Sector Analysis of the Folkeskolen Area).

Economist (2004), "Home-schooling: George Bush's Secret Army", *The Economist Print Edition*, 26th February.

Flatley, J., H. Connolly and V. Higgins (2001), *Parents' Experiences of the Process of Choosing a Secondary School. A Nationally Representative Survey of Parents of Children in School Years 5, 6 and 7*, DfES, London.

Hirsch, D. (2002), "What Works in Innovation in Education, School: A Choice of Directions", CERI Working Paper, OECD/CERI.

Hirschman, A.O. (1970), *Exit, Voice, and Loyalty: Responses to Decline in Firms, Organizations, and States*, Harvard.

Lambert, C. (2002), *Access to Achievement. Opening up Good Schools for All*, London, Adam Smith Institute.

Ministry of Education, Culture, Sports, Science and Technology (2003), School Basic Survey, Japan.

MORI (2004), *Open Access to Education*, available: *www.suttontrust.com*, December.

IEA (2003), PIRLS 2001, "International Report: IEA's Study of Reading Literacy Achievement in Primary Schools".

Putkiewicz, E., A. Wiłkomirska and A. Zielińska (1997), *Szkoły społeczne i szkoły państwowe. Dwa światy socjalizacji* (Civic schools and state schools. Two models of socialisation), Społeczne Towarzystwo Oświatowe.

Sági, M. (2004), Az iskolaválasztás oksági modellje a racionális cselekvés elmélet alapján, in Judit Lannert, *Hogyan tovább? Pályaválasztási elképzelések Magyarországon*, Országos Közoktatási Intézet, Budapest, Hungary.

Taylor, Nelson and Sofres (2003), *Public Perception of Education*, Summary report, TNS, London.

Zawadska, B. (1992), *O czym milczy prasa? Analiza dyskursu oświatowego w prasie ogólnopolskiej i regionalnej* (What is avoided in the press? The analysis of educational discourse in national and regional press), Warsaw University, Department of Sociology; master thesis written under the supervision of Professor Renata Siemieńska.

Chapter 4
PARENT AND COMMUNITY "VOICE" IN SCHOOLS

This chapter investigates parental and community influence as exercised on running schools. Decentralisation is bringing decision-making closer to the local and school levels, but countries differ in the extent to which parents are regarded as partners or external to the school. The country evidence shows that formal opportunities of involvement are not necessarily translated into actual influence. Many parents complain that their views are sought only on practical issues. Parental engagement tends to decline as their children grow older and even some countries with high reported parental interest are finding declining involvement over time. Low involvement can reinforce the view on the education side that parents are external to school life. As in many organisations, the active parents are not necessarily representative of the parent body as a whole, with the less well educated and disadvantaged under-represented.

The most direct way in which demands can be expressed is not through "exit" and choosing an alternative but through the direct exercise of parental and community influence on the running of schools. This chapter examines the exercise of "outsider voice" in schooling, including what is reported by countries about how active parents are in running schools and how they are involved in the formal channels to participate in the decision-making process. It points to the reported shortcomings in the ways this form of voice is exercised, which may partly explain why exercising choice may often be seen as a more effective means of ensuring that schooling corresponds to demands. It is also the case that exercising voice can itself be highly demanding if that entails becoming closely involved in the running of schools – exercising choice periodically may well be a simpler alternative for many busy parents.

A useful introduction to the issue of voice is given by comparative figures on the extent to which decision-making is devolved to the school level or whether the key decisions are made higher up. The general trend to decentralisation notwithstanding, Figure 4.1 shows that there is very wide variation between countries in the extent to which decision-making has become a local matter. England, New Zealand and especially the Netherlands are unusual in the very high proportion of decision-making now residing with schools, while others such as Greece, Australia, Mexico and Luxembourg still rely on the central education authorities for the majority of their decision-making.

Figure 4.1. Percentage of decisions relating to public sector lower secondary education, taken at each level of government (2003)

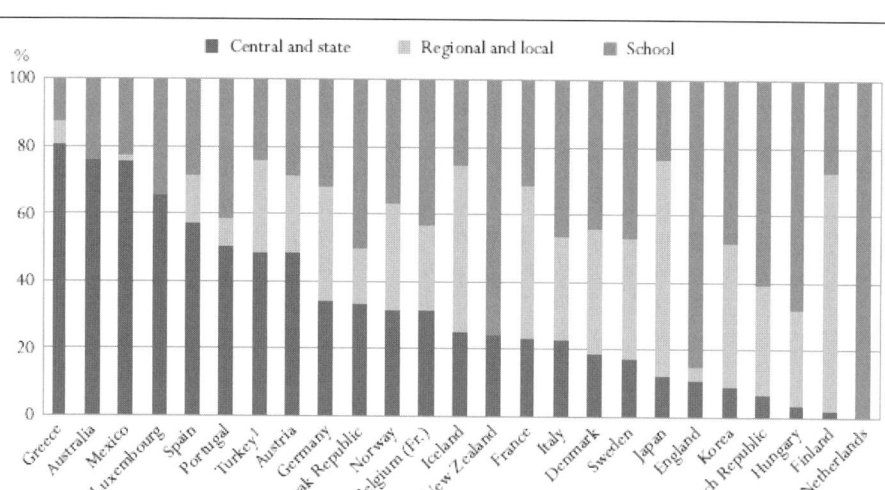

1. Turkish data refer to primary education only.

Countries are ranked in descending order of the percentage of decisions (on issues like organisation of instruction, personnel management and planning) taken at central and state levels of government. Example: In Greece, 80% of decisions are taken at the highest level of government (central and state), 7% at regional and local levels and 13% at the school level.

Source: *Education at a Glance – OECD Indicators 2004*, OECD, Paris, Table D6.1.

The formal exercise of parental voice in schools

The evidence from various countries raises interesting issues about how far parents want to exercise a role – and which role – in schools, and whether they feel that they have a "voice". Most countries have made provisions for parents to receive information about schools. In the different countries surveyed for this study, provisions have been established for parents to participate in school decision-making. Some of these are rather formalised and refer to parent associations and parent councils, *i.e.* elected bodies of parents. School councils, on which elected parent representatives serve together with teacher representatives, are a more recent development in most countries. They tend to have more influence than parent associations and often have a say in developing local curricula, deciding about budgetary matters, and recruiting and selecting teachers and principals. However, there is a serious issue regarding how many parents are familiar with these arrangements and which parents these are, as well as the extent of involvement in formal procedures for governance.

A number of the country reports describe the formal changes towards extending parental powers or, as is the case in Denmark, where parents have long played an essential role in the running of schools, including the *folkeskolen*. In 1990, the parents' role in school decision-making was further strengthened with the creation of boards of school governors. Each board consists of five or seven parent representatives elected by all parents whose children are enrolled in the school. In addition, there are two representatives elected by and from among the school's employees and two student representatives, so that parents are in the majority. The board of governors develops the guidelines for a school's activities, approves the school budget and decides curriculum and staffing matters. According to 2001 evidence described in the background report, Danish parents are very committed to their children's schooling and on average spend three hours a month at the school.

In England, there have been radical changes in the governance of schooling over the past 10-15 years, with enhanced powers at the centre combined with much greater autonomy of decision-making by schools themselves. Each maintained school has its own governing body representing a wide range of different individuals and interests. Governors, between 9 and 20 per school, are volunteers and elected or appointed depending on what stakeholder they represent. Parent governors are elected by parents, staff governors by staff members, and additional community governors are appointed by the governing body. Governors fulfil three essential functions: they are to provide a strategic view, act as critical friends, and ensure accountability. Governing boards are involved in decision-making in a wide range of areas. They manage the school budget, make curriculum decisions, and they report a school's examination results to parents and others. They are in charge of drawing up an action plan after an inspection. Governing boards also play a core role in staffing a school, dealing with new appointments, staff appraisal and grievances. Given the very significant responsibilities now extended to parents and local communities in England through these governing bodies, it is useful to consider how well this "voluntary" form of governance actually works.

In Finland as elsewhere, the increasing significance of parents in school development is related to the strong trend towards decentralisation to the local level. The new Basic Education Act from 1999 requires schools to be developed in co-operation with parents. The fact that schools draw up their own curricula, guided by the broad framework of the National Core Curriculum, has also brought school operations closer to parents (Niemi, 2000). Forms of co-operation between home and school include parent-teacher meetings, school festivities, parents' meetings, discussion events and one-to-one discussions between individual teachers and parents. In common with Finland, decentralisation is a key aspect of the Polish situation. Increasing decentralisation during the 1990s resulted in growing parental interest in the quality of schooling. In response to problematic conditions in schools, parents began actively to shape educational policy by creating school councils and associations to collect funds for improving conditions in schools. Parent and student representatives on the School Council (Educational System Act 2000) can in theory exert considerable influence over schooling.

A framework for parent and student involvement has been in place in Austria since the 1970s and there was a move towards greater school autonomy in the 1980s. Parents in every class elect a parent representative and those parents elected vote for parent representatives delegated to a body consisting of teacher, parent and student representatives which is chaired by the principal. In Slovakia too, parents' associations are independent and voluntary bodies which provide the school with feedback about learning and teaching and in some cases supply the school with additional financial resources. Since 2000, elected school boards consisting of parents and other community representatives control the management of a school and the work of a school's employees. Parents are involved in the development of school profiles. Slovakian schools are now entitled to add classes to their curricula according to the interest of students, parents or the region. At present, more than 40% of the primary schools organise additional teaching of mathematics, sports or foreign languages, music or arts on the request of parents.

Spanish parents can participate in the steering and management of schools through parent associations. There are currently two parallel parent associations: the secular Spanish Confederation of Parent Associations (CEAPA) and the National Catholic Confederation of Parents (CONCAPA) representing mostly Catholic parents, especially those whose children attend Catholic private schools or *centros concertados*. This confessional parent association has been politically influential, campaigning for the right of parents to select the education they consider appropriate for their children. About 65% of the parents of students in primary education and 58% of the parents of students in secondary education are fee-paying members of one of the parent associations.

In Japan, recent policy initiatives have focused on greater parent and community involvement in school management. The newly introduced "school councillor system", which can be established by local education boards at their discretion, aims to promote the co-operation of community residents and parents in the life of the school and to make the plans and achievements of the school management accessible to a wider public in order to create stronger accountability. School counsellors also contribute to external evaluation and quality development. In addition, Japan has created provisions for the establishment of so-called community schools, which are sensitive to local needs and co-managed by community representatives who recruit the school principal through an open-application system.

A further possible way in which parental voice can be exercised in school life is through the use of surveys of opinion. Since the second half of the 1990s, for instance, many Hungarian schools have begun to conduct parental surveys as part of quality assurance systems of schools (Györgyi and Török, 2002). Parents – and in many cases students – are asked about their views on the school. The needs and satisfaction of parents and students are monitored more or less regularly in the 20% of schools where a quality assurance system is introduced. So far, however, survey results are only used informally and receive only restricted publicity.

Decentralisation is the natural context for the discussion of enhancing parental and community voice in school decision-making but it is far from synonymous with it. Consistent with the patterns in Figure 4.1 decentralisation may simply be about shifting the locus of decision-making and administration from one government level to another. Even enhanced school-level powers do not automatically mean that the "external" voice will be listened to. On the positive side, even if parents do not have voice, decentralisation facilitates diversity and in doing that may facilitate choice as an alternative way to make the system more demand-led. Focusing on formally recognising parents in decision-making, the brief overview of developments below shows that the results are mixed, going further in some countries than others.

Perceptions, patterns and problems regarding parental involvement in school governance

There are some positive reports from parents in the country cases regarding the opportunities to participate in school life. The majority of parents in England felt either "very involved" (38%) or "fairly involved" (51%) in their children's education (Moon and Ivins, 2004). Women were more likely to feel involved than men. In a survey on parental involvement in education, Williams, Williams and Ullman (2002) found that nearly 30% of parents felt "very involved" in their children's school life and another 56% "fairly involved". The main reported barrier to involvement was work commitments (cited by 53% and 33%, respectively). Other factors were child-care difficulties and lack of time. Three-quarters of parents (Williams, Williams and Ullman, 2002) said that they would welcome greater involvement. About a fifth of parents reported having helped out in class at some point (28% in primary schools and 12% in secondary schools). Other types of involvement included fund-raising and special interests, such as sports and drama.

In a 1998 Austrian study by Eder, parents were asked to report about and to assess their experience in the interaction with schools and teachers. Almost all forms of interaction concerning organisation of events and projects were assessed positively, and also experience regarding problems relating to achievement and to health and related issues. Only one issue, scheduling, was reported with negative examples only. Research conducted in Finland suggested that parents' attitudes towards co-operation with schools were positive. In a survey carried out by the National Board of Education (Apajalahti and Merimaa, 1996), almost all primary school rectors reported that parents had participated in preparation of the curriculum. About 70% of schools had provided parents with an opportunity to participate in setting objectives for students and in student assessment.

Despite these positive perceptions, however, the country reports indicate that there are problems with parental engagement in school life. Partly, this is about the actual level of engagement. There is declining involvement the higher the level of schooling and age of the students. In Finland, for instance, when students move to the lower secondary level, co-operation between home and school often fades away, despite both parents' and schools' wishes to the contrary (Virtanen and Onnismaa, 2003). In Hungary, active parent involvement is strongest at the initial stage of schooling and in alternative schools (Golnhofer, 2001). Parents of primary school age children in England are more likely to feel involved than those of secondary, and mothers more than fathers (Moon and Ivins, 2004). Despite the strong membership of parental associations in Spain, the great majority of parents do not actively participate in the association's work. According to a 2002 survey (INCE), in primary schools only about a quarter of the parents become actively involved in school issues; in secondary education the proportion is even lower at 15%. Membership of parent associations is higher among parents of children in private schools than of those in public schools, but surprisingly the proportion of those parents who become actively involved in school issues is slightly lower in private schools.

Through-time trends may also be worrying for expectations of high parental engagement, and remove any simple thesis of a secular trend towards greater stakeholder participation. Some reports refer to the possibility that active participation is actually falling over time, even when the interest is there. In spite of the high level of interest that Danish parents take in their children's schooling, for instance, participation in school boards is in decline. The turnout in the elections to school governing boards has fallen consistently from 43% in 1990 to 31% in 2001. The proportion of contested elections has gone down from 43% to 14%, and only one in four board members stand for re-election for a new term. It remains to be analysed whether declining involvement leads to declining influence, or whether involvement is declining because influence is limited. In Spain too, according to the national report, some parents even question the real purpose of school councils and the level of parents taking part in school council elections is low with a decreasing tendency in recent years.

There may be perceived problems even when parental participation has gone up. In Finland, for instance, a report by the National Board of Education on the development of student assessment stated that primary schools had experienced an increase in co-operation between home and school and in parents' active involvement (Apajalahti and Merimaa, 1996). But it also highlighted another problem: teachers did not feel that they had received enough training to facilitate that co-operation. Even in this case, there seem to be significant problems: Niemi and Tirri (1997) found that, according to both teachers and teacher trainers, co-operation with parents was among the ten most poorly achieved objectives. Parents in Finland also complain that responsibility for the activities had been left to just a few parents (Siniharju, 2003).

This judgement about the role played by relatively few parents is far from unique to Finland, including in some of those countries reporting positive findings. Data from Austria, for example, show that with regards to access to information, participation and decision-making, there seems to be a marked difference between parents' representatives and the broader body of parents. While parent representatives feel well informed and respected by the school, Eder *et al.* (2002) found tensions in the relations between the wider group of parents and the schools.

Across all countries, there are the familiar equity issues regarding *who* is most likely to be those exercising their "voice" in the affairs of the school, especially in the more fundamental issues concerning school educational policy. Women are more likely to perceive themselves to be involved in their children's schooling than men. A study by Metso (2004) in Finland suggests that co-operation between home and school was more active at those schools where students' parents had a higher level of education. This study shows that the parent dealing with the school was usually the mother. According to the English research review by Desforges and Abouchaar (2003), the extent and form of parental involvement is strongly influenced by family social class, maternal level of education, poverty, maternal psycho-social health and single parent status and, to a lesser extent, ethnicity. This is complemented by a report by Ofsted, the English school inspection agency (2002), which reached the important if unsurprising conclusion that governing bodies were found to be more effective in areas of socio-economic advantage. In Hungary, poorer parents stay away from school meetings, and one reason suggested is so as to avoid having to contribute finances for extra-curricular programmes. Communication between schools and Roma parents is a particularly severe problem (Liskó, 2001), with one-fifth of Roma parents having no contact to the schools their children attend at all. Immigrant parents in Spain participate at a comparatively lower rate which is according to a report by the Spanish Ombudsman (2003) due to a lack of language skills rather than – as many teachers suggest – a low level of interest in their children's schooling or a low educational level.

These are issues about the gap between activists and the rest, which are found in general in social organisations as well as the equity issues about *who* tends to concentrate among the activists. There is also a gap between the structures that could in principle exist for parental participation and the extent to which they actually exist – a problem of implementation. Although the authority of the school board has been continuously expanded in Hungary very few schools have effective school boards in place. Despite a legal provision calling for their creation, school councils do not yet exist in most Polish schools because parents themselves would have to take the initiative of founding them. School councils can be created by a motion from at least two of the three democratic bodies functioning at a school – teachers', students' or parents' councils. But the national study reports that school councils only exist in one in ten Polish school and indeed many of them have stopped working, usually because of representatives of teachers' councils withdrawing, often under pressure from principals. Where the school council does not exist, its duties tend to be performed by teachers' councils. Even in Finland not all educational institutions which may have a board actually do so: according to a government survey, just over half the schools providing basic education or general upper secondary education do not have one.

There are thus some problems apparent concerning how parental participation – through which demand may be expressed – works in practice including: declining engagement in higher levels of schooling, the gaps between the activist parents and others, the lack of preparation of teachers to engage with parents and others, and even lack of structures themselves (the gap between the theoretical possibility to exercise influence and actual practice). To look behind these problems, there is a set of factors which may represent a "vicious circle" in some countries and settings – the combination of low interest from too many parents and the limits to the voice that schools are willing to extend to parents. These are partly matters about legal frameworks, but more especially they are about cultures of co-operation. Switching to more demand-led schooling is much more easily said than done.

Low parental interest and lack of influence over fundamentals – a vicious circle?

Parents in some countries believe that the issues on which their engagement is sought are the relatively simple, practical ones rather than fundamentals about the school and education. Some of the reports suggest that the level of interest of parents, in both practical matters and fundamentals, is low, compounded by possible active discouragement by the school. There is reference to the worrying possibility that some parents are discouraged by the perception that their children may be put into a vulnerable position if they take a critical stance on matters of school policy. The more that these observations are true, the less can it be said that demand finds a direct expression at school level through voice as opposed to the indirect expression which comes from choice mechanisms in the educational "market place". Even if parents are involved but it is on the minor matters regarding school events and local fund-raising, this is scarcely evidence about exercising a say which is tantamount to shaping "demand". It is more accurately seen as participating in ensuring the supply.

These limitations to voice can be seen in sharp relief in the developments of Central and Eastern Europe. It may well be that the long experience with "supply-dominated" systems has engendered a culture which discourages parental involvement. In Hungary, only about one third (36%) of the parents said that they had a good or a very good influence on pre-school or school education while the majority said that they could hardly influence the education of their children because schools do not involve them (Gallup, 1999). More educated parents articulate their needs better, they have a more critical attitude towards education. Similarly, in the Czech Republic, the new obligation to establish school councils with equal representation of local administration, parents and education staff has run into difficulties of implementation because of the low interest among the parents. In the case of Slovakia, the number of parents wanted to be directly involved in the management of the school is "negligible". Relatively few parents claimed their right to participate in the selection and evaluation of teachers, decision-making on what lessons the child would be taught at school, co-decision-making on the development of school system in the area of their residence, to participate in the teaching lesson and decide on the broad focus of the teaching.

Polish findings show both the relatively limited range of issues which engage parents and the low overall levels of engagement. In Poland, 20% of parents in rural areas and 15% of parents in cities held some function on a school's council or a parents' council. Half of those "active" parents call for more rights to exercise influence on schools. But, most Polish parents are interested in issues that seem to be limited directly to their own children's education. One survey (CBOS, 2000) indicated the current priorities and interests of Polish parents to be: setting the level of a yearly paid voluntary contribution to school (92%), organising school trips and other events (91%), solving difficult educational problems with individual students (85%), influencing schools' important financial decisions (77%), organising extra and additional classes (76%), creating the school's pedagogical programme, and influencing the choice of educational methods (65%). Some schools, most of them private, allow the educational programme to be developed co-operatively by the different bodies functioning at school but the level of parents' involvement is still rather low: (Polish Ministry of Education, 2001) 76% of primary schools and 80% of *gimnazja* studied parents' expectations before creating their school programme but only 25% of parents say that they were actively involved in the process of creating the programmes. A lack of procedures for democratic election and organisation of parent representative bodies and the strong political influence of local politicians and authorities over schools are seen as major obstacles to parental participation.

According to a 2000 survey in Denmark, parental influence on the content of teaching is limited to helping to shape the schools' social culture, including the social rules of the school. Thus, despite the long tradition of fostering school-home co-operation, Danish parents still have no particular influence on the content of teaching. However, the findings seem to indicate that they generally do not want it either. A survey conducted in Austria (Eder, 1998) is also not sanguine about untapped parental demand for greater involvement. It revealed that less than half of the parents in Austria want to have a say in matters of schooling. Currently, 30% of the parents say that they are "strongly involved" in matters of schooling, 20% are "clearly not involved". The 1999 Education Monitoring (IFES, 1999, p. 52) claims that 40% of parents want to have greater influence on school decision-making. According to Eder's 1998 survey only between 20% and 33% of parents want to be involved in school decisions, but only some issues – like developing the school profile, deciding about school events and about sanctions – are of interest to them. Very few parents want to be involved in the selection and assessment of teachers and principals. More recent research by Eder *et al.* (2002) suggests that parents feel that their opinions about schooling and teaching are not taken very seriously by teachers and that critical feedback to the school might have negative consequences for their children.

Spanish legislation from the 1980s laid down parents' and students' right to participate in the control and management of schools through the School Council chaired by the school principal. In theory, School Councils are involved in formulating a wide range of issues on the school's agenda: its pedagogic programme, the development of rules and regulations, adopting and assessing curriculum and extra-curricular activities, monitoring academic performance, and any further development of the school's infrastructure. In reality, however, many parents feel that the agendas in School Councils are largely set and dominated by teachers and that parental scope for decision-making is limited to minor issues such as the organisation of school events and largely excludes key areas of schooling such as the content of the curriculum and the evaluation of school effectiveness. The Spanish country report laments a general lack of communication between parents and schools and a lack of information about the potential role of school councils among parents.

Hence, the problems clearly go well beyond questions of parental apathy or their busy lives, and relate also to how welcome they feel as partners in the educational enterprise. Many teachers in Hungary still disapprove of the fact that an "external actor" (the parent) has a say in school life. Similar to the case of Austria, some parents fear negative consequences for their children when expressing their opinions about a school. Parent-teacher associations which have been in place for decades are mostly seen as service organisations to the school, to help in organising school events and trips; most teachers regard the parents in these associations as assistants rather than stakeholders.

Since the late 1990s, each educational institution in Hungary has been obliged to develop and implement its own educational programme, including an analysis of the school's situation, curriculum guidelines and the school curriculum. Slightly more than 60% of the local school boards entitled to approve the educational programmes said that there had been discussions with school principals concerning the content of the educational programmes. According to a national school principals' survey, parents and students are hardly involved in defining the content of education. More than 50% of schools involved parents in the analysis of situation by asking them to give their opinions but less than 10% provided opportunity for parents to contribute to the development of the educational programme, lesson schedules and curricula. In recent legislation, Czech schools are now obliged to develop a school curriculum decided upon by their school councils, but we have noted how problematic councils have been to set up. Where councils exist, a third of the council members will be representatives of the founding body, normally the municipal self-governing authority, one third representing parents and senior students, and a third for teachers. It is expected that this will lead to more public influence over the content and methods of schooling.

This section raises as many questions as it answers concerning the existence or not of a "vicious circle" between low parental interest, on the one hand, and unwelcoming or "unbending" schools, on the other; in any case, this will not be a constant across systems and communities. However, the evidence paints a picture of problems and pitfalls to be overcome. Even in the countries with some positive indications from the evidence (Denmark, England, Finland), there is little to suggest that an opposite "virtuous circle" is in place. And, even where home-school cooperation is the rule, the question still arises as to whether this is primarily as a vehicle to express parental demand(s) or else to assist the functioning of the school – to assist rather than to influence or actively to change.

Exercising broader stakeholder voice and the curriculum

In many countries, education is being decentralised with the aim *inter alia* of creating more local stakeholder influence on schools. A balance is being sought between some form of national curriculum and local freedom in creating the curriculum. There is no straightforward relationship between the degree of centralisation and room for stakeholder influence – even if a curriculum is centrally designed, consultative processes may give stakeholders a chance to exercise voice; where there is decentralisation in practice the role of stakeholders in the creation of a curriculum may be limited. There is a range of practice from the country reports which sheds light on other forms of parental and stakeholder "voice" beyond formal involvement in school governance.

For instance, several forms of consultation are normally used to aid the development of the National Curriculum in place in England since 1988.

This curriculum sets out a statutory entitlement to learning for all students – it determines what will be taught, sets attainment targets for learning, and determines how performance will be assessed. The consultation includes advisory groups, public consultation and focus groups. In 1997, for example, the central Department set up an advisory group to advise the government on the aims and purposes of citizenship education. Membership of the advisory group included teachers, lecturers, politicians, representatives of voluntary organisations and others. Groups consulted during the enquiry included schools, voluntary organisations, charitable foundations, church organisations, trade unions, local authorities, universities, government agencies and departments, organisations in other countries and individuals. Recently, there have also been attempts at listening to students "as educational experts".

In Finland, the National Board of Education decides on the national core curricula for pre-school education, basic education and upper secondary education and on the national requirements of competence-based qualifications. The national core curricula include the objectives and core contents of different subjects, as well as assessment principles. The local education authorities and the schools themselves draw up their own curricula within the framework of the national core curriculum. Parents and representatives of the professional community are involved in the design of local curricula. Vocational institutions establish local networks to become involved in regional business life. Local providers have opportunities to decide on the ways in which co-operation with parents and representatives of the local community is to be implemented. Parents also take advantage of this opportunity, though it is difficult to estimate the precise extent of their opportunities to influence the preparation of curricula.

A number of stakeholders is involved in the development of new curricula in Austria which requires a highly formalised process, including the social partners and the parents' and students' representative bodies. The process is mainly run by a selected group of subject experts, administration and teachers. Regulations about school autonomy have given more discretion to schools, which can now involve community partners in decision-making. Danish legislation stipulates minimum numbers of lessons for school subjects and the framework for a number of optional subjects as well as the central knowledge and proficiency areas that apply to the subjects. Municipalities have, for a number of years, had the opportunity to prepare local curricula but only very few municipalities have taken this opportunity. Recently, there has been a trend for increased central control to ensure increased focus on academic performance at *folkeskolen*. In 2002, threshold targets were introduced for years 2 and 7, as well as final goals for years 9 and 10. The Hungarian example also shows that in spite of a decentralisation of developing educational profiles and contents, the formal role of parents, students and employers may still remain limited. Only about 20% of vocational training schools in Hungary discuss curricular issues and requirements with employers and chambers. Likewise in the Czech Republic, the curriculum for basic education has been developed by independent teams of experts and by experienced teachers. The contribution of groups representing civil society and parents was small. Even teachers, with the exception of active teachers associations focusing on reform, were not particularly involved.

In the United States, recent developments seem to go against the current in the other countries (Plank, 2005, p. 11). Efforts made in the past years to raise standards, equalise opportunities and strengthen accountability have reduced the scope for local decision-making in education. The increased importance assigned to standardised assessment, for example, has resulted in a steady standardisation of curricula. By and large, schooling has moved from being a local issue to becoming a battleground on which larger political battles are staged. This development has had major implications for the role of local stakeholders. Parents who might once have voiced their concerns at a local school board meeting must now enter a larger political stage.

General discussion

The general tendency is to give more discretion to local authorities as well as parents and other stakeholders of schools at the local level. Most countries recognise the diversity of demand and have created mechanisms allowing the "clients" of education, to express their interests with regard to the provision and the structure of schooling. When changes are examined on the basis of detailed examples, however, the notion of the shift to "demand-led" schooling is complex and problematic. The material reviewed in this chapter does not allow us to arrive at any clear-cut conclusions but it does suggest that the complexities arise from both the parental and the school sides of the equation.

At the school level, most systems have sought to become more participatory, with formal opportunities for parents to raise their voice and influence schooling. A broad trend has been towards a combination of more autonomous schools and increased stakeholder – most importantly parental – participation in decision-making. But this has gone hand-in-hand with more intensive steering from the centre in some cases, showing that there is no simple relationship between governance and influence. Moreover, the formal opportunities are neither always implemented nor necessarily translated into actual influence. Various reasons were mentioned in this chapter. Parents are not always aware of the possibilities they have to influence schools. In some countries establishing a formal body for different stakeholders to help run schools requires initiative which is not always acted on. Another barrier is the fear that if they raise critical issues about schooling this might negatively affect their child. Parents' lifestyles and work lives may militate against intensive involvement, but there may also be many parents who are simply not interested.

The chapter has discussed a possible "vicious circle", where low parental involvement reinforces negative views from the education side that parents and the community should have only a very limited say in what goes inside schools. This is clearly a subject that could very usefully be illuminated through further research. It would be very useful to more accurately ascertain how far there is genuine interest or its lack among parents in being closely involved in decision-making at school level, on which issues, and how open to change this is if they perceive greater opportunities to exercise voice. Similarly, it would be very useful to clarify how open are the doors of schools – wide and welcoming or simply just ajar? Research can also usefully help to clarify the costs that come with wider participation and not only the benefits.

There are practical questions concerning how to create more effective parental participation. Removing barriers is important: at the most basic level this means that that all parents are informed about their rights and opportunities to have a say. School leader and teacher professional development may be needed. It may be possible to find alternative ways to consult parental opinions. Organising regular surveys or consultations at the national, regional or local level in which parents are asked about a number of major issues is another possibility. It will however be important to ensure that such consultation is genuine rather than cosmetic, for if there is widespread consultation with no impact on provision or the system it might reinforce cynicism, not participation. We have already observed in Chapter 2 that the knowledge base concerning attitudes and expectations tends to be weak; even where it is more robust, there is no simple relation between the findings and the decision-making process.

The broader context of governance is important here. The greater the decentralisation which enhances school-level autonomy without a concomitant increase in local participation the more worrying is the possibility of a "democratic gap". This is the accountability argument for parental involvement. When the state takes full responsibility the minister is directly answerable to Parliament. This direct responsibility is weakened with decentralisation especially as it extends to the school level (Figure 4.1 illustrates how important this is in some countries). How far this is perceived to be an issue of democracy in turn relates to how schooling is itself regarded, legally and culturally, in any country. How far is local decision-making regarded as a matter of effective administration rather than a subject for the legitimate exercise of local democracy? How far does the notion of "demand-sensitive" or even "demand-led" enjoy any currency in a system? Or, are the checks and balances operated in other ways, such as through central authorities retaining firm guideline powers or inspection or through the "marketplace" of choice mechanisms?

The limited parental participation in school decision-making is compounded by the fact that the parents who do participate are not representative of the parent body as a whole. The fact that parents with certain backgrounds (white, middle class, higher educated) tend to be over-represented among the activists becomes more of a problem the more that their decisions serve limited self-interests rather than those of the whole student body. If, on the other hand, the skewed social representation does not significantly alter the direction of parental voice, it might better be viewed as an imperfection rather than a major flaw. The point to be underlined here is that while there are well-rehearsed arguments about the equity risks of enhancing the role of parental choice, enhancing voice is not free from the same concerns.

This is an issue which arises as much at the centre of the system in the consultation which takes place over curriculum and assessment issues as it does on the ground. Do the representatives of the middle-class viewpoint tend to favour choices and priorities based on the traditional academic values, which may serve neither their own children well nor those from other backgrounds? We have also seen in the previous chapter the importance of the effective organisation of voice to raise its "volume" for specific interests and parents. Again, the social differences in the way this is exercised might be the price to be paid for greater democratic participation in education but voice has as much a social dimension as does choice.

We return thus to the question of demand. This chapter has focused on parental, and to some extent community, voice as a key route through which demands may be expressed. The shortcomings in the arrangements for parental participation in governance are an alert to the fact that such expression is by no means assured. We have also noted that education systems differ fundamentally in the extent to which they aim to be more "demand-driven". They differ in the extent to which schooling is regarded as a crucible for local democratic politics as opposed to national decisions and values. But we have also seen that parental participation in education is not always about making their "demands" heard – involvement is not always about voice. Often it is to be more informed about their child's progress and to assist in the learning process. It is often to help ensure the effective functioning of the school as an institution, being part of the "supply" not just "demand". On many questions parents may want to leave it to the professionals, not as a matter of apathy but as one of trust.

Hence, the role demand plays and the extent to which it finds active expression in school provision is not determined by the fact of parental involvement in the life of the school. It is also about how far genuine "partnership" (OECD, 1997) is in place. It is about whether the dynamics of education systems are essentially closed and self-determined or instead open to external influence. While there are risks involved in any changes, it seems likely that the long-term trend is towards greater openness. Education systems which embrace this are likely to find themselves with greater influence through partnerships rather than be overtaken by voices and choices which discard the views of the professionals.

References

Apajalahti, M. and E. Merimaa (1996), *Raportti peruskoulun oppilasarvioinnin kehittämiskokeiluista vuosilta 1994–1995* (Report on experiments into development of student assessment at comprehensive school, 1994–1995), National Board of Education, Helsinki.

CBOS (2000), *Educational Reforms – The Level of Information and Support*, Warsaw.

Central Council for Education (1997), "The Model for Japanese Education in the Perspective of the 21st Century".

Desforges, C. and A. Abouchaar (2003), "The Impact of Parental Involvement, Parental Support and Family Education on Pupil Achievement and Adjustment: A Literature Review, Research Report 433, DfES, London.

Eder, F. (1998), *Schule und Demokratie*, Studienverlag, Innsbruck.

Eder, F. *et al.* (eds.) (2002), *Qualitätsentwicklung und Qualitätssicherung im österreichischen*, StudienVerlag, Schulwesen, Innsbruck.

Fuller, B. (2003), "Education Policy under Cultural Pluralism", *Education Researcher*, Vol. 32/9.

Gallup (1999), *Gallup vizsgálat a pedagógiai minőségértékelés mai helyzetéről*, Összefoglaló kutatási jelentés, *www.gallup.hu/Oktatas/Release/Gq/pedmin990504.htm*.

Golnhofer, E. (2001), *Az oktatás tartalma, az iskolák belső világa, a tanítás és a szocializáció intézményi szintű kérdései*, Vitaindító előadás az OKI konferencián.

Györgyi, Z. and B. Török (2002), A Comenius 2000 minőségbiztosítási program a résztvevő oktatási intézmények tapasztalatainak tükrében, kézirat, Oktatáskutató Intézet, Budapest.

IFES (Institut für Empirische Sozialforschung) (2003), *Bildungsmonitoring*, Research reports commissioned by the Ministry of Education, Science and Culture, Vienna.

INCE (2002), *Sistema estatal de indicadores de la educación*, Ministerio de Educación, Cultura y Deporte.

Kurt Lewin Foundation (2002), Alapítvány kutatása, Survey of Kurt Lewin Foundation, OJBH.

Liskó, I. (2001), A cigány tanulók és a pedagógusok, *Iskolakultúra*, December, pp. 3-14.

Metso, P. (2004), *Koti, koulu ja kasvatus. Kohtaamisia ja rajankäyntejä. Helsinki: Suomen kasvatustieteellinen seura.* (Home, school and education. Encounters and boundaries), Finnish Educational Research Association, Helsinki, abstract available in English.

Moon, N. and C. Ivins (2004), *Parental Involvement in Children's Education*, Research Report 589, DfES, London.

Niemi, H. (2000), "Vanhemmat ja koulu uutta yhteistyötä etsimässä", in U-M. Ekebom, M. Helin, R. Tulosto (eds.), *Satayksi kouluongelmaa. Opettajan käsikirja* ("Parents and schools in search of new co-operation", in *101 school problems. A teacher's handbook*), Edita, Helsinki.

Niemi, H. and K. Tirri (1997), *Valmiudet opettajan ammattiin opettajien ja opettajien kouluttajien arvioimina. Tampereen yliopisto* (Teacher proficiency as evaluated by teachers and teacher educators), University of Tampere.

OFSTED (2002), "The Work of School Governors" (HMI 707), Report from HMCI, Ofsted, London.

OMBUDSMAN (2003), Informe: La escolarización del alumnado de origen inmigrante en España: análisis descriptivo y estudio empírico, Vol. I and Vol. II, Madrid.

OECD (1997), *Parents as Partners in Schooling*, OECD, Paris.

Polish Ministry of Education (2001), *The Social View of the Reform. Education 1997-2001*.

Siniharju, M. (2003), *Kodin ja koulun yhteistyö peruskoulun alkuopetusluokilla. Yhteistyön arvostus ja toteutuminen Helsingin kaupungin peruskoulujen alkuopetusluokilla lukuvuosina 1983–1984 ja 1998–1999* (Co operation between home and school in the first two years of comprehensive school. Appreciation for and implementation of co-operation in the first two years of comprehensive school in the city of Helsinki during the school years of 1983–1984 and 1998–1999), Helsinki University Press, Helsinki.

Virtanen, N. and J. Onnismaa (2003), Kehityskeskustelut kodin ja koulun yhteistyömuotona (Performance discussions as a form of home-school co-operation), *The Finnish Journal of Education*, Vol. 34, 4, pp. 351-358, abstract available in English from *www.jyu.fi/ktl/abs2003.htm#nrod*

Williams, B., J. Williams and A. Ullman (2002), *Parental Involvement in Education*, Research Report 332, DfES, London.

Chapter 5
WHAT DO THE STUDENTS SAY?

This chapter examines students' perceptions and expectations of schooling, albeit on the sketchy evidence base in most countries. Schooling is seen as important for its social aspects, learning and getting ahead in life. In many countries there is overall satisfaction, though complaints tend to focus on the relevance and interest of courses. These complaints grow as students get older. Girls tend to be more ambitious and readier to face challenge than boys. High expectations are correlated with geographic residence, socio-economic status, and parental education attainment, especially the mother's. On choice, the chapter mentions some information from secondary education on the room to choose between different subjects around the compulsory core school curriculum. It also looks at exit behaviour through absenteeism. The opportunities for students to exercise their voice are in general limited and not always seen as effective. Students tend to regard being listened to and engaged in their lessons as the more important aspect of voice.

Demand critically involves the students themselves. If they are saying that what school has to offer means little or nothing to them, then it would be hard to claim that it is "demand-led". At the same time, it is a moot question how far students know what they want and are able to exercise mature judgement. How far is or should what students say they need be something different from their parents' wishes? How far should the individual projects of learners and their families be the guide as opposed to the broader collective projects of countries and communities which may not appeal to particular individuals? These are some of the questions now raised acutely by the aim of "personalising" education as mentioned in Chapter 1 (see OECD, 2006a).

This chapter does not examine "student demand" in the sense of "participation" which is how the term is often used to refer to the greater number or fewer of a generation staying on in education or choosing a particular track. Instead, we cover what young people are saying they want from education, how they experience it, and how those attitudes and expectations are patterned variables, including by gender and social background. These questions in turn raise others for policy about how much intelligence there is in education systems in terms of knowing what young people report on these matters. We begin with an overview of the international picture and discussion of expectations (where data are not extensive), before turning to student satisfaction and their positive or negative judgements about schooling where data are relatively rich. We then explore – in parallel with the chapters on parents – the notion of student voice in schools.

The broad international picture

All education systems aspire not just to transmit subject knowledge but also to prepare students for life in general. The views of the majority of 15-year-olds suggest that education systems are quite successful in this respect. Typically, students in the OECD countries agree that school helped give them confidence to make decisions and has taught them things which could be useful in a job. Nevertheless, a significant minority of students, 8% on average across OECD countries consider school a waste of time. An average of 32%, and above 40% in Germany, Hungary, Luxembourg, Mexico and Turkey, report that school has done little to prepare them for life. In many countries, students' attitudes towards school vary greatly from one school to another, suggesting that school policy and practice can be influential in addressing this problem (PISA 2003, first results). Such findings are arresting and, when particularly negative, disturbing. But as we suggest below it is not straightforward for students still in school to give a rounded appreciation of how the experience will have benefited them at a later time.

Less problematic are student reports about how they experience school. In general, they report a positive sense of belonging at school. On average across OECD countries, 81% of the students agree that their school is a place where they feel like they belong. Eighty-nine per cent agree that their school is a place where they make friends easily. The overall figures do not support the thesis of a majority of teenage students feeling disgruntled and disaffected, even if they make up a significant minority in some countries (PISA 2003). Figure 5.1 has two dimensions – sense of belonging and attendance level. It shows just how wide are the variations between countries. The OECD countries that stand out as those where the sense of belonging is lowest at over 30% or more are Poland, the Czech Republic,

France, Belgium, Korea and Japan, especially Poland and Korea at over 40%. Countries where low belonging is lowest are Sweden, Ireland, Hungary, and the United Kingdom at below 20%. It also shows that there is no clear relationship between participation in school and a sense of belonging, with some of the countries where reported engagement is lowest enjoying among the highest participation levels (notably Korea and Japan). ("Sense of belonging" is based on students' responses to six items describing their personal feelings about being accepted by their peers and whether or not they felt lonely, "like an outsider" or "out of place". The second component is "participation", which is measured by the frequency of absence, class-skipping and late arrival at school during the two weeks prior to the survey.)[1]

These wide variations among countries found in the PISA data of 2000 are confirmed by the PISA data gathered in 2003: students in Austria, Germany, Iceland, Luxembourg, Norway, Spain, Sweden and Switzerland report the highest sense of belonging at school. In contrast, the lowest sense of belonging at school is reported by students in Belgium, the Czech Republic, France, Japan, Korea, Poland, the Slovak Republic and Turkey. For example, while in Sweden 5% of students report that school is a place where they feel awkward and out of place, more than three times this proportion report that feeling in Belgium and Japan (PISA 2003, first results).

That there are countries notable for having a low sense of belonging, while high attendance and indeed high achievement, indicates that there are complex relationships between the perceptions of young people, social pressures to participate, and the ingredients of academic success. It would be particularly useful to focus especially on the countries which manage the combination of high belonging, high attendance and engagement, and high achievement at the same time. The dimension of how schooling is experienced by young people is an important additional element to that on achievement levels alone.

Another country noted for its high achievement, Finland, does not differ essentially from the OECD average on the indicators of engagement and participation, as confirmed in Figure 5.1. But, in most OECD countries, the

---

[1] Sense of belonging and participation: There are two issues concerning the validity of participation measures that warrant discussion. One is that the measure of participation could be more extensive, what was measured in this study is narrowly focused on student absenteeism. Part of the problem is that the very nature of school participation varies considerably among countries, making it difficult to measure participation with a broader focus that includes time spent on homework, participation in classroom discussions and involvement in sports and other extra-curricular activities. Second, the construct itself undoubtedly has a cultural component and thus varies among countries and among subgroups within countries.

likelihood of having a low sense of belonging and a low participation rate are clearly greater among students from low socio-economic backgrounds. In Finland these differences are small – social class influences attitudes less (OECD, 2003).

Figure 5.1. Prevalence of students with low sense of belonging and low participation

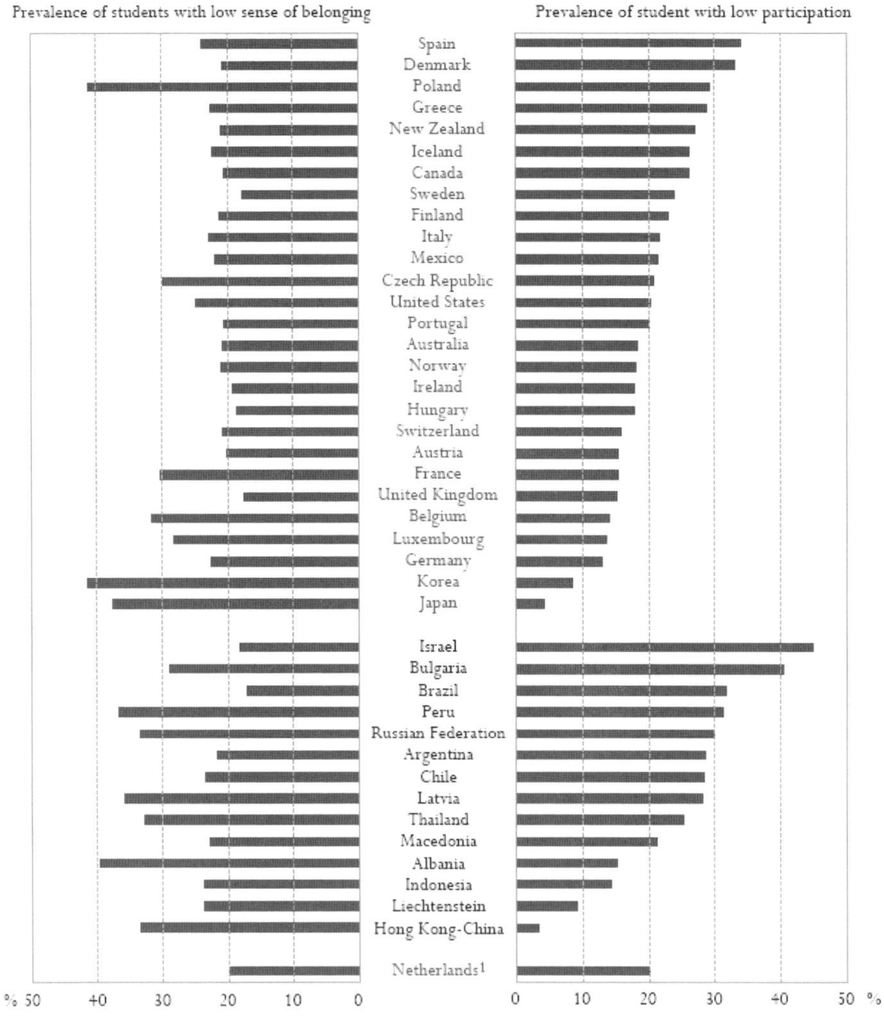

Prevalence of students with low sense of belonging   Prevalence of student with low participation

1. Response rate is too low to ensure comparability.

Source: OECD (2003).

What do young people expect from school and how satisfied are they?

What do the national case studies have to say about young people's attitudes towards schooling in terms of their expectations, aspirations and satisfaction? On expectations, some of the most insightful data are from Poland. *Gimnazjum* students have high expectations of their school, both about being well prepared for further education and about additional activities offered by schools to give them a chance for developing their interests, for entertainment and social contacts (Konarzewski, 2001). The aspirations are manifested in more seeking a longer education – more young people choose secondary schools after which they can continue education at higher level.

Research conducted from 1993 to 2002 on what motivates young people in Poland to study shows significant changes connected with the change of economic situation. In 1993 most of those questioned pointed to the possibility to get a well-paid job (66%). Less important were: independence and self-reliance (37%), easier life (36%), interesting job (36%), intellectual development and self-fulfilment (34%), and in sixth position there was avoiding unemployment (16%). By 2002, this last argument had gained ground among those questioned (46%), together with well-paid job (73%) and easier life (42%). Those who selected to get an interesting job did not change (36%), fewer of them chose independence and public respect and recognition as important motivating factors (13%) and the biggest decrease was observed at intellectual development and self-fulfilment (13%) (CBOS, 2002). The need of economic security became more important than gaining the non-material benefits of education. Economic ends play an important role in shaping the demands of young people, especially in changing circumstances where this value of education becomes reinforced.

During the decade covered by this research, the number of young people who believe that in 10 to 15 years' time they will be highly educated had more than doubled to nearly 60%, and at the same time a decreasing number of people plan to finish their education after the end of the upper secondary cycle. A large majority of general secondary school students are confident that they will get a university education (96%) and students of technical and profiled secondary schools think the same (78% and 77% respectively); around 20% increase in this respect since 1996. A 1990s UK review (Keys and Fernandes, 1993) noted that many students believe that an important purpose of school and education is to help to get a job or to set them on the path for their chosen career. Around 90% agreed or strongly agreed that schools should help them to do well in examinations, teach them things that would be useful when they got jobs, and to be independent. When asked the question, "Thinking about the future, what are the most important ways your school could help you?", most of the students' responses are concerned with preparation for the future. The main issues mentioned were: the acquisition of life skills, such as self-discipline, motivation and independence; the provision of support and encouragement; the provision of knowledge about careers; the provision of high quality education; help in gaining qualifications for further study and help in gaining qualifications for employment.

Most young people in the United States aim to complete secondary school and enrol in post-secondary education. According to Public Agenda (1997, p. 11) "few see any alternative path to an acceptable future". The educational aspirations of African-American and Hispanic youngsters are not significantly different from those of whites; indeed, "black and Hispanic teenagers believe even more strongly than white teens in the advantages of a sound academic education" (*op. cit.*, p. 32). What seems to be underlined by this and the other examples is that student expectations – realistically perhaps – are very conventional. They do not necessarily share an equal emphasis on what is important as their parents. Among the 12- to 17-year-olds surveyed in Japan for the 16th World Youth Survey, for instance, while the items of "specialist knowledge" and "skills to be used in employment" are supported by 47% and 31% respectively of the parents as a main reason for going to school, they are less supported by students (18% and 15% respectively), while to gain an "educational record and qualification" is supported by both parents and students (42% and 37%). What young people are looking for, the emphases and nuances apart, is very similar to that sought by their parents and the wider public; perhaps this is a sign of how effectively schools socialise pupils with similar aspirations as the wider population.

But this is difficult terrain, conceptually and empirically. Students may give answers to those conducting surveys about their fundamental beliefs regarding the purposes of education, but more realistically they attend school because it is a convention and obligation for them to do so. How far is it realistic to expect that they will have a rounded, coherent appreciation of what education can give them in the future before it has happened, rather than afterwards? The notion of "expectations" could thus be more difficult to apply and interpret for those currently in school compared with those who have already completed it and moved on. This is not a reason to ignore the student voice on the grounds that it is immature but to focus especially on where student experience is direct and where perception is most likely to shape behaviour. In the next section, we look at what the study reports had to say concerning the patterns of school student aspiration and the more detailed evidence concerning satisfaction.

Patterns in educational aspirations and choices

Those most confident that they will attain a university degree are the young people living in cities and towns who describe their families' economic status as at least average. Girls tend to be more ambitious than boys. For the Czech Republic, the PISA data confirm higher female aspirations and show a strong link between parents' education and the socio-economic status of the family and students' aspirations. Over 70% of students who do not aspire to pass *maturita* have a mother who did not graduate, and around half of students with this low level of aspiration are students with the lowest socio-economic status who make up a quarter of the cohort (Straková *et al.*, 2002). Selective schools are attended by students with higher socio-economic and cultural capital who enjoy higher study aspirations. Students with average reading literacy from families with a lower social status who study at six- and eight-year *gymnázia* have far higher aspirations to study further than lower-level secondary students of the same age. An overwhelming majority of *gymnázia* students plan university education, but the same applies to only half those in secondary technical programmes with *maturita*. According to the 1999 IEA study on citizenship education, almost all students in the Czech Republic believe education is an important precondition for success in the labour market. Lower-level secondary school students are, however, far more sceptical – or more realistic – than *gymnázium* students as regards the prospects of self-fulfilment.

In a Hungarian survey of students' workloads (2002), every tenth student answered that the nearest school for them would be the best one, the others voted in equal proportions (45-45%) for where they feel best or where it is the easiest to continue studies. Background, however, makes a difference to the responses. In the higher grades of general secondary schools to continue to further education is the most important aspect for some 6 in 10 students, although half of vocational secondary school students also mentioned this as the most important aspect. Gender differences are also clear: boys prefer the easier, more convenient solutions while girls are more ambitious. The strongest is the link to parents' educational attainment: those coming from the most educated families chose the "further education" response two and a half times more than those coming from the least educated ones. In Hungary, for both rural and urban students the chances of further studies beyond secondary education increase with the level of school performance. More rural than urban youngsters with better school performance choose vocational training institutions; town children choose upper-level secondary school more than their village counterparts (Lannert, 2004).

Children of more educated parents choose universities not only due to greater material security but also because in these families the norm of further education is stronger. A survey conducted in 1999 with 17-year-old Hungarian students suggested that that there is no difference between the aspirations of weaker students by family income if the school attainment level of the mothers is the same. Further education aspirations differ more by the school attainment of the mother than by family income: material capital cannot be exchanged in a simple way for cultural capital.

Teenage school students make the connection between schooling, their level of education and future opportunities in the labour market. They see the necessity to get a good education in order to continue their education, go into higher education and successfully enter a labour market that is perceived to be ever more demanding. Young people living in urban areas tend to aim at the university level more often than those in rural areas. In this case, supply might be shaping demand: the fact that urban areas offer a better infrastructure for higher learning and a more diverse labour market will most likely create ambitions and provide role models for ongoing learning.

Students' satisfaction with schooling at different levels

The picture from the national data reported for this study confirms that of the international overview, while adding detail and different groups to the PISA 15-year-olds. They show that the overall satisfaction level with schooling is generally high across the countries studied, but there are differences between countries, and by level of schooling and the gender and background of the school students.

The majority of students in England appear to like school (Keys and Fernandes, 1993; NOP Consumer, 2003; Keele, 2004; MORI 2004). Keys and Fernandes found three-quarters or more of 11-year-olds and of 13-year-olds agreed or strongly agreed with the statement "On the whole, I like being at school". Students were even more likely to believe that their own school was a good school. According to the Austrian school monitoring survey, students' overall satisfaction with schools is similar to that of the wider population (IFES, 2003, pp. 9–11). A poll in Poland (SOURCE) found that 82% of primary school students said they liked their school and two-thirds said they had many friends (only 12% said they felt lonely at school), and 76% of students expressed positive opinions about their teachers. In Hungary one fifth of 7th-graders liked going to school very much and more than two-thirds of those surveyed had a positive attitude to going to school. Students' attitudes to school in Finland are positive regardless of the school subject (National Board of Education).

The situation in Japan is more complex for the PISA studies show them with a consistently low level of engagement and high participation while the Japan Youth Research Institute (2002) reported that nearly 8 in 10 are happy with their school life. Nevertheless, a high 38% of them feel that "school life presents a great challenge to them" and, despite their low actual absence, 65% of the students surveyed "want to be absent from school", 74% answer that they "want to skip lectures" and 72% "feel dissatisfied with the ways of the school they attend". Those who feel that they want to skip lectures or to stay away from school increased over the 20 years to 2002.

There are clear differences in reported satisfaction by age of school student in England. The Children and Young People Survey (NOP Consumer, 2003) reported that 87% of primary school students and 68% of secondary school students agreed that their school was "really good". NOP Consumer (2003) noted that the majority (over 80%) of primary school pupils said that they enjoyed being taught by their teachers, agreeing that they were always fair, listened carefully to them, were kind and caring, made them work hard and made lessons interesting. Similarly, Keele (2004) found that over 90% of primary school students reported liking their class teacher and that about two-thirds of secondary school students said they enjoyed being taught.

In the Czech Republic, 69% of the students in grade four said that they liked their school (IEA, 2003). This study also showed that positive attitudes to school are less frequent in higher years of compulsory schooling. Among 11-year-old students 24% do not feel happy at school, the same holds true for 34% of 13-year-olds and for as many as 41% of 15-year-olds (Provazníková *et al.*, 2004). Concerning the level of satisfaction with the choice of a secondary school in 1999, 86% of secondary school students in the Czech Republic said that they were happy about their choice. Over half said they would choose the same school and programme again. *Gymnázium* students tend to be happier with their choice than students in secondary technical schools and secondary vocational schools. Many more *gymnázium* students also believe that their school is excellent (56% compared to 18% of secondary vocational students). An overwhelming majority of *gymnázium* students (97%) agree that the school provides them with relevant knowledge.

In the PISA surveys, about two-thirds of Austrian students say they are satisfied with their schooling environment. Vocational colleges are rated highest among Austrian students, schools accompanying apprenticeship training are rated lowest, academic secondary and vocational schools are rated at a similar level in between the two. The upper-level schools are rated positively in more dimensions than the lower-level ones. In the first year of upper secondary education in Hungary there are slightly more students who like going to school than among those who are two years younger. Among general secondary school students there are twice as many students who like going to school than among vocational training schools students. Among vocational students those studying economics, commerce and ICT have a more positive attitude towards school than those studying in industrial or agricultural vocational secondary school and their attitude is even more positive than that of 4-grade general secondary schools students (Survey on students' workloads, 2002). Slovak Republic research (Beňo and Beňová, 1994) reported the students of secondary grammar schools like going to school much more than students at vocational schools. School is mostly liked by primary school pupils but 24% of them nevertheless say that they dislike school. Most students of vocational schools (40%) go to school without anxiety. On the whole, positive evaluations prevail over negative ones, even if in the Slovak Republic one student in four dislikes going to school, every fifth student attends with anxiety, and 15% of the students say that they attend school without any interest.

Spain is one of the countries where the general level of student satisfaction is lower than some of the other countries covered here, with only about 70% of Spanish students saying that they feel satisfied with their school (Ombudsman, 2003). This is especially apparent at the secondary level. Concerning students' perception of school functioning, in primary education, 82% of the students were satisfied in contrast with only 53% in secondary education. Only a very small minority – around 5% – expressed a high degree of dissatisfaction with learning in their school. The majority of students said that their teachers liked them very much, just 10% answered negatively. As might be expected, students in primary education expressed more agreement with their teachers and what they learn than secondary students.

In Finland, good learning outcomes are related to more positive attitudes, with the relationship stronger in the higher than in lower grades. Attitudes are more negative among older than among younger students but then they are more positive among students among the oldest ages in school who move on to upper secondary school compared with those continuing in vocational education and training. Attitudes among the small number of students who do not intend to apply for upper secondary education on completion of comprehensive school are the most negative of all. There is a very small group of students, even in Finland, whose attitudes towards school are very negative.

Gender and other population differences in reported satisfaction

In England as in other countries, girls are more likely than boys to like school and their teachers, enjoy schoolwork, and perceive their own school as a good one. They are less likely than boys to perceive schoolwork as boring (Keys, Harris and Fernandes, 1995; Keele, 2004; MORI, 2004). The assessment by girls of their school experience in Spain is also more positive than by boys (Ombudsman, 2003). PIRLS data (2001) in the Czech Republic suggest that while an already-high quarter of the girls (24%) do not like their school, this is much higher among the boys (38%). Other surveys confirm the higher percentage of boys who dislike school. A WHO survey on "Health Behaviour in School-Age Children" (1998) shows similar results for older students. When asked whether they like and feel good at school, over one third of the boys and one quarter of girls gave a negative answer. Gender differences vary stereotypically by subject area in Finland (National Board of Education) in that attitudes towards mother tongue, the second national language (either Finnish or Swedish) and foreign languages, geography and biology are more positive among girls than boys; boys on the other hand have more positive attitudes towards mathematics, physics and chemistry.

In Hungary, positive attitudes are also more prevalent among students who are more successful at school and those who come from more privileged backgrounds, with fewer who do not like going to school at all, with the opposite among Roma and other minority students and among boys. Students in Spain who attend schools with more than 30% of immigrant students are more satisfied with their school than those at schools with a lower proportion of immigrant children, a possibly unexpected result. Immigrant children express about the same level of satisfaction (71%) as non-immigrants. Eighty per cent of Spanish students stated that they were satisfied with the contents and the process of learning with again immigrants showing the same or even more pronounced approval (85%). In England, white students were more likely to think their school was good (MORI, 2004). The attitudes of immigrant and ethnic minority students in particular need further clarification.

In sum, in all the countries covered, student attitudes to schooling are generally positive, although older students are more critical about schooling than younger ones: primary school children are more satisfied than students in secondary schools, with those at the lower secondary level more than student on the upper level of secondary education. These findings are in line with international research on students' enjoyment of learning in schools which gradually decreases with age. Learning in primary schools is less overshadowed by the pressure to get good marks to be able to continue one's education or successfully enter the labour market. Education in primary schools tends also to be more experiential, offering greater opportunities for students to follow their natural curiosity and be engaged in their own learning. In all the countries covered students in higher educational tracks tend to be more satisfied than students in vocational education.

Absenteeism – students voting with their feet?

Absenteeism is a more direct and extreme expression of student dissatisfaction and disengagement. Given the patterns of satisfaction, it is not surprising that absenteeism rises significantly between the primary and secondary levels. In England, the average rates of unauthorised absence are significantly higher in secondary than in primary schools. Only a minority of students take unauthorised absence. About 16% of primary students and 23% of secondary students had at least half a day's unauthorised absence in 2003/04. Such students missed, on average, eight half-days in primary schools and 15 half-days in secondary schools during the school year (DfES, 2004). About half the parents in England perceive bullying as a problem and just under half consider truancy levels to be problematic (Shaw, 2004). Studies by Keys and Fernandes (1993) and Keele (2004) found that younger students were slightly less likely than older students to admit their absences, and that girls were less likely to report that they did so (Keys, Harris and Fernandes, 1995). These two last findings seem to be consistent across countries and with the patterns of school satisfaction.

Over half of Danish students state that bullying takes place in their class but it does not seem to increase or decrease as students progress through school (Jacobsen *et al.*, 2004). In Poland, according to PISA data, 41% of the surveyed students said they had experienced the feeling of loneliness and isolation in school, and 29% admitted having arrived late and having played truant. Research on rates of absenteeism in compulsory schools shows that it is very much an age-related phenomenon. The average number of unexcused absences is one per primary school student and 13.2 per *gimnazjum* student (Konarzewski, 2001). The problem is bigger among rural than urban students.

In a 2002 survey (NHK), 17% of Japanese junior high school students and 25% of the senior high school students answered "often" or "sometimes" to the question "How often do you feel like not going to school?". In Japan, the number of absent students increases with age – especially between the first and second grade in junior high school, and between the first grade in junior high school and the 6th grade in elementary school. However, as we noted in Figure 5.1 there is a wide discrepancy in Japan between experiencing disengagement and lower participation. One in every 275 elementary students (0.36%) and one in every 36 junior high school students (2.8%) are classified as long-term absentees, which is very low indeed even if it has risen rapidly in junior high schools in recent years. The following problems are seen as reasons for truancy: lack of self-esteem, increasing numbers of children who do not see they have any future prospect of vocation and profession, lack of motivation toward studying, and lack of a sense of obligation to have to go to school. In many cases, student absenteeism is explained by students not wanting to go to school because they fear being bullied.

In the United States (Plank, 2005), there is a substantial number of young people whose engagement in schooling falls short of publicly articulated norms and standards. Some of these young people remain enrolled in school, but are only weakly engaged in educational pursuits. Many others drop out of school before completing secondary education. This brings a variety of problems, both for the young people themselves and for the broader society, especially as drop-out is concentrated among young people from marginalised or disadvantaged groups, including urban students and members of racial and linguistic minorities. There are significant gender differences in educational performance and educational attainment, and these are increasing with time. Boys are significantly more likely than girls to drop out of school; young women are more likely than young men to enrol in post-secondary education and to complete post-secondary degrees. Gender differences are especially pronounced among African-American and Hispanic young people; for example, more than 60% of the bachelor's degrees awarded to African-Americans are awarded to women.

In each country, there is a minority of students whose attitudes to schooling are very negative, though as shown through the satisfaction data this minority can be a large one, including in some countries with high levels of attainment and achievements. The likelihood of truancy increases with the age of a student and is more common in the last years of secondary education. In all countries, female students like school better than males do, and absenteeism is significantly higher among boys. English evidence suggests that there might be some under-reporting among girls and younger pupils, where the source of data is self-report, which would amplify these differences.

Educational factors that students identify as shaping their attitudes

What do students say about schools which might lie behind their positive or negative attitudes? They do not have a one-dimensional understanding of what schooling is about and schools represent many different things to them: as places to learn, to meet friends, and to get credentials to get ahead in life. Their expectations and attitudes are shaped by many factors beyond the formal provision of education. The reasons most cited by Japanese students for going to schools were "good friends". Among the 12- to 17-year-olds, 80% cited this as their main reason (16th World Youth Survey). For students in the Slovak Republic, schoolmates are important for one third of students of secondary grammar schools, one fifth of students of specialised secondary school and a little less for students of the other schools. They are slightly more emphasised by boys than girls. "Good and friendly relationships among schoolmates and decent behaviour of the schoolmates" is also appreciated. As well as solidarity, friendship, openness, interest in the other gender, good team, the effort to help each other, possibility to speak openly about problems, being happy, having fun, having a chance of a good chat, no abuse of younger by the older, possibility to relax after a tough day at school. They like a good atmosphere, comfort, openness at school, resulting from, for example, interesting discussions with the teachers on various issues, good relationships among the students, mutual help, willingness of the schoolmates, feeling secure, substantially free, having free, informal discussions with the teachers, vividness, music and singing.

For students in Austria, the most important quality criteria from the students' perspective are the social competencies of teachers and the individualisation of teaching. Other very important criteria are modern instructional methods, technical equipment and a diverse range of subjects (IFES, 2003). Other English research indicates that students particularly appreciate teachers with good interpersonal skills and teaching ability (Morris *et al.*, 1999). In Denmark, an indication of what students would like at school is the charter of the national students' interest group. Schools should offer a good environment with teaching "that makes sense to students" and take responsibility for students' personal development, take individual students into account and provide "room for everyone", use evaluation methods to help each student improve his or her performance, provide students with an understanding of and commitment to democracy, facilitate co-operation between students, school and parents. During the 2002 meeting of the Danish Children's Council the children expressed four aims of schooling. In addition to friends and a good physical and mental environment, these were good teachers and alternative education methods. Environmental factors featured also in the list of complaints about school made by the Slovak school students, as they include the amount of sitting at school, lack of moving, air, physical activity and little leisure time as well as concerns about the teaching.

United States students participating in the Public Agenda survey (1997) identified a variety of obstacles to achieving their educational objectives, including disruptive peers, low standards and expectations for student behaviour and performance, and bad teaching. The results display "a yearning for higher expectations and closer…monitoring by schools and teachers" (*op. cit.*, p. 23), reflecting the recognition even among young people themselves that they could accomplish far more in school than their teachers now require them to do. In Spain, according to survey results about adolescents' view of their last three months at school (CIS 2003), only 3.4% of the Spanish teenagers surveyed said that they were "bored" and 15% felt "stressed". According to a Hungarian study conducted by Aszmann *et al.* (2003), nearly one third of the 6 000 students asked find school difficult (35% of 5th-graders, 37% of 7th-graders, 40% of 9th-graders and 30% of 11th graders). Slightly higher is the proportion of students who are fatigued by school. The ratio of these students increases from grade to grade (in grade five this ratio is 37%, in grade nine 47%).

Some of the reasons given to MORI (2004) by young people in England who did not enjoy education suggest ways that schools do not meet their needs. Half of those who did not enjoy school said they would like lessons to be more interesting; nearly 40% would like more choice over the subjects they studied and over 20% would like more practical or vocational courses. These data might indicate that educational approaches to cater to individual student interest by personalising learning (OECD, 2006) have not sufficiently been applied in the schools examined. Morris *et al.* (1999) in their literature review concluded that aspects of work-related learning, especially work experience, were viewed positively but that students often criticised the content and delivery of the mainstream curriculum.

Keys and Fernandes report that, although 55-60% of 11- and 13-year-olds said they found their work interesting in all or most lessons, a minority (about 9%) perceived all or most of their lessons to be boring. The students taking part in the study by Keele (2004) were even less enthusiastic: though about 60% of 11- to 16-year-olds agreed that schoolwork was at least fairly interesting, about a third considered it to be boring; another study (NOP Consumer, 2003) found even higher levels at about a third of 7- to 11-year-olds and 44% of 11- to 16-year-olds agreeing that schoolwork was dull and boring. The majority of lower secondary school students in England reportedly appreciate the value and importance of schoolwork *per se*, however, even if they are less convinced by their own lessons. Keys and Fernandes found a large majority (over 90%) of 11- and 13-year-olds believing that schoolwork was worth doing; only a tiny 3% agreed or strongly agreed that the work in all or most lessons was a waste of time or that school itself was a waste of time. So such total rejection is rare, but several studies (for example, Keys and Fernandes, 1993; Keys, Harris and Fernandes, 1995; Keele, 2004) have identified a minority of around 10% of students who hold consistently negative attitudes towards school and schoolwork.

This relates back to those singled out earlier in this chapter who "vote with their feet" to express dissatisfaction: the young people who are regularly absent from school. The most common reasons cited for truancy from school are boredom, problems with teachers, bullying and peer pressure. According to the 2000 PISA data on the Czech Republic, even students in the more demanding *gymnázia* say they were bored (about 50%) and a quarter did not want to go to school. This is surprising given that *gymnázia* as selective schools are regarded as better meeting the needs of talented and inquisitive children than lower-level secondary schools. When asked why they do not like their schools, 64% of primary Polish school students said that they were bored (The Social View of the Reform, 2000). Among *gimnazjum* students 23% described the level of boredom as higher than in primary school and 37% said it was at the same level (Konarzewski, 2001). English students who disliked school tended to consider schoolwork boring, unimportant and a waste of time, to dislike their teachers, and to behave badly in class (Keys and Fernandes, 1993). Disaffected students also tended to be less likely to have a positive academic self-image, to perceive their parents as supportive, and to hold positive views on the ethos of their school. In addition, Morris *et al.* (1999) in their literature review noted that poor relationships with teachers were often associated with disaffection, disruption and truancy, and to have a negative effect on attitudes towards staying on at school.

Morris *et al.* (1999) cite research reporting that absentees do not necessarily dislike school: of those involved, only about one third indicated that they disliked schools. However, those regularly absent often disliked their lessons – the desire to avoid a particular lesson was much more frequently given as a reason for truanting than a desire to avoid school. This might indicate that it is not the culture or climate of schools students want to "exit" but rather particular ways that learning is organised within the school. Most absentees (Malcolm *et al.*, 2003) said that the reason they wanted to miss school was boredom, and over half said they were not sorry afterwards. School-related reasons for truancy were thought to be more important than home-related factors by secondary school students and parents – they perceived the main causes of truancy to be bullying, problems with teachers and peer-pressure. Students also cited problems with lessons and social isolation.

With regard to the content and methods of teaching, young people express a preference for active, participatory learning and would like to see more opportunities to gain practical work experience. Teachers are most appreciated for good social and interpersonal skills and the ability to pay attention to individual student's abilities, interests and needs. By the same token, there is a widespread viewpoint that school is "boring", or more particularly too many lessons are not interesting enough. Dislike of lessons, especially particular lessons or individual teachers, can mean that the disenchanted become more permanently disengaged. Given that the social aspects of schooling tend to be relatively positively appreciated by young people, this suggests that a great deal about engagement with school hinges on the quality of the in-school, classroom experience.

The expression of student voice

But what about students having a "voice" in order to express their demands as part of the educational process – this can also be seen as an important component of any school system that purports to be "demand-led"? This section both discusses the more generalised perception of having a "voice", and the more specific, formal opportunities for voices to be expressed. It does not add up to a picture of students clamouring for greater participation, even if this characterises an activist minority.

Findings from England on students' views on participation in the classroom are not very consistent. Clear majorities of students in England wanted parents and children to have at least some say over what is taught in schools – 87% and 74%, respectively (Park, Phillips and Johnson, 2004). Slightly more young people agreed than disagreed that students were too young when they had to choose subjects to specialise in (*ibid.*). Students frequently express a preference for active participatory learning. Evidence for students' preference for participatory learning was also found by Keys and Fernandes (1993), according to which lower secondary school students were more likely to say that they liked lessons where they were actively involved with others or where they made things than lessons where they worked alone.

Regarding individuality at Danish *folkeskolen*, the democracy survey (Jacobsen *et al.*, 2004) shows that: students widely feel that they can be themselves at school and 8 out of 10 feel that they are able to be themselves in class, so acquiring a foundation in democratic practice that is central to a liberal outlook. Students feel they have good opportunities to express their opinions: 8 out of 10 students think that they can do so even if they disagree with the teacher or other students in the class. The opportunities increase as they progress through school: 86% of students feel that there is a good feeling of class community and only 8% say they are not included; which is equivalent to 1-2 students per class. Three-quarters feel that they are good at working together in class. The students also indicate that discussion of disagreements makes a positive contribution to the discussion culture. A survey (2002) of around 1 200 students from year 6 carried out by the Children's Council shows that only around 20% of students are often or always afraid to express their opinions out loud in class.

The Danish democracy survey shows that students have varying perceptions of their influence in the classroom. Students' opinions are split when it comes to the legitimacy of participation in decisions concerning the academic content of lessons. Some students say that they do not consider it desirable to be involved in decisions concerning teaching as such involvement would obstruct effective learning, while others take a very positive view of having an influence on teaching. They state that the involvement of students both instils a feeling of responsibility and is motivating of learning. The majority state that they are unable to change how they are taught and under a third feel that they often have an influence on teaching. The survey by the Children's Council also shows that meaningful forms of participation seem not to be widespread, as 54% of students are never or seldom involved in setting their own work plan, 90% of students never or seldom have the opportunity to choose the books with which they work, and 58% of students are never or seldom involved in choosing topics.

More Austrian students want to have more say on school issues than their parents do but this is still a minority demand whether from students or parents (41% students as compared to 18% parents). Those issues where students want to have more say are in matters which concern their every day life: around three-quarters mention the organisation of school events and the shaping of their recreation area; about 4-5 in 10 mention school regulation, the school canteen, influence on passing grades for students at risk, and teacher assessment. The more organisational and school policy related items, such as selecting staff, decisions about learning content, including the decisions about disciplinary measures, were mentioned by about one third of students or less.

As part of a study entitled "Youth in the Czech Republic" (2002), secondary school students said that they feel they can speak up on classroom-related matters, but most of them (61%) think they do not have a say in decisions at school level. The results of the IEA Citizenship Study (1999) also revealed that the confidence of Czech students and interest in active participation in addressing school-related problems is lower compared to many other countries. Two-thirds of secondary school students were positive as to having an opinion on school issues, and 60% were involved and interested. Students at six- and eight-year *gymnázia* are more active in this respect than lower-level secondary school students.

Students in the Slovak Republic clearly lament a lack of participation in their schools and see the freedom of expression as limited. Asked about what they would change in schools if they had the power to do so, students responded that they would like to have discussions in their lessons, and would like to be asked for their opinion about schooling. They want teachers to be fair, to create a good atmosphere at school and to provide students with more rights and the freedom to express their opinion and to speak openly. Many idealistically would like students to be given the right to select their teachers and to create their own education programme. They would like to be able to act more responsibly; extra-curricular activities would play a more important role and additional lessons and study groups would help weaker students. Class size would be reduced, school premises would be utilised in the interest of students, and the curriculum harmonised with the needs of practical life.

The formal representation of student voice

As regards more formalised ways of involving students in decision-making, most countries have done more to promote parent participation than that of students. Opportunities for student decision-making with regard to important issues are limited. Where they exist they are not always seen as effective. The existence of student councils and other representative bodies can be an important means to provide a schools' student body as a whole with a voice to articulate concerns. The effectiveness of student councils is, however, affected by the teachers in charge and their commitment, which seems to differ widely. It is also affected by the general culture of participation and listening to "student voice" – where such a culture is weakly established it will not be surprising if formal structures are not taken seriously by the majority of students.

Danish secondary students are guaranteed direct influence on the teaching itself via legislation stipulating that the choice of methods and material must take place as far as possible in co-operation between teachers and students. In addition to this, a number of provisions guarantee students' involvement in decisions of individual significance – for example, teaching in optional and elective subjects, year 10, special teaching, etc. If a school has year 5 or higher students, the students may form a students' council. Students are represented on the school's board of governors. Three-quarters of students in Denmark consider that the students' council is important or very important for the school (the proportion decreases up through the years). However, 64% of students feel that the students' council has little importance for them personally, and this proportion increases in the older years. Although a large majority considers that the students' council is important for the school, they do not see it as a place where they can "voice" their very personal demands and concerns about schooling. As justification for their scepticism, students state that their council makes decisions on insignificant matters, the decisions are very protracted, and that the teachers do not take it seriously. The influence of the students' council is said to depend critically on the contact teacher – too often the teachers are perceived as unenthusiastic and the council's work is left to the students with little impact on teachers and school administration.

In England, formal ways in which students can participate in decision-making in schools are the establishment of schools councils and the appointment of students as associate members of school governing bodies. A survey of schools carried out as part of the BT Citizenship Research Project (BT, 2003) reported that 86% of the schools surveyed had established schools councils. They are forums that give students a chance to say what they think about how the school is run. Members of a school council are normally elected by their peers to represent a class or year group to discuss issues raised by students through class representatives and year group councils. Since 2003, school governing bodies have been able to appoint under-18-year-olds as associate members. These students can attend meetings and be members of governing body committees, although they do not have voting rights (Hallgarten and Breslin, 2003). In Japan, the chance of the students' participation in school management is now opened through the policy of external evaluation which sometime includes students as evaluators in the schools. Although there are no Czech data as to the number of schools with student councils or parliaments, the proportion of active students is far lower in the Czech Republic than the average of the 28 participating countries in the study on citizenship and democracy (IEA, 1999): only 13% of students were sometimes involved in student council or parliament activities, while the international average was 28%. The proportion is higher nevertheless in six- and eight-year *gymnázia* (20%).

From this discussion, we can speculatively propose three conclusions regarding "voice". First, students are not very demanding about having greater say; they might even be described as surprisingly compliant. Hence, theirs tend not be unrealistic demands which might threaten the nature of schools as institutions and be impossible to concede. Second, though any strict comparison is difficult on the basis of this evidence, school systems do seem to differ as regards how ready they are to listen to students. This is a matter of general culture in a school system which is very difficult to quickly change, at least as much as it is about individual practices in schools and classrooms. Third, it is difficult to see how students can truly engage in their schooling unless they are being listened to since exchange is at the heart of learning, not transmission.

General discussion

This chapter has focused on a key population group – the students – rather than a conceptual element in the framework underpinning this study. Information on their expectations and satisfaction is sketchy in most countries, though there is some data available from international sources, like PISA and the IEA studies. There may be a perception that this sort of "subjective" soft evidence is inherently inferior to the firm "hard" measures such as class size, teacher qualification level and so forth. Such a hard-nosed view where it does prevail leads to only limited understanding of how education can be improved. It is at odds with any ambition to move from an essentially technocratic "supply-led" perspective towards one which is much more informed by "demand", *i.e.* the views and wishes of the various stakeholders being served by education.

The country material indicates that students have a multi-dimensional understanding of what schooling is about. School is at the same time a place to learn, to meet friends and to get the necessary credentials to get ahead in life. Regarding their satisfaction, the limited data reveal several tendencies across countries: students are fairly satisfied, although older students are less satisfied than younger ones; students in higher tracks are more satisfied than students in lower tracks; girls are more satisfied with schooling than boys. The general perceptions of school by students are, then, broadly positive albeit with a larger or smaller minority of students who plainly hold more negative assessments.

The social environment of school, friendships, and the peer group are clearly important determinants of the positive viewpoints, to such an extent that school can be an attractive place to attend even when its manifest purpose – teaching and learning of the curriculum – is not well achieved. With regard to the content and methods of teaching, students express a preference for active, participatory learning and would like to see more opportunities to gain practical work experience. Teachers are most appreciated for good social and interpersonal skills and the ability to pay attention to individual student's abilities, interests and needs. All of this is "personalisation" of method rather than necessarily of curriculum. Regarding content of teaching students tend to be most critical about the schools' ability to prepare them for changing labour markets, namely to teach ICT skills, modern languages and teamwork.

There is a widespread viewpoint that school is "boring", or more particularly too many lessons are not interesting enough. It may be that school is anyway now out of tune with the current generation of students[2]

---

[2] This issue will be explored in the "New Millenium Learner" project of OECD/CERI.

who grew up surrounded by technology so that, no matter how hard it tried, it would be found wanting. The enthusiasm of many students belies this pessimistic conclusion – the quality of the teaching, the personalisation of methods, and the interest of content can make the critical difference. The evidence concerning how dislike of lessons, even a particular lesson, can be telling for the vulnerable to become more permanently detached warrants particular attention: a relatively small but negative experience can have lasting consequences. Listening to student voice may be both individual teachers listening to individual students but also the extent to which the broad messages from the student population about quality, interest and methods are being listened to by the system as a whole.

All of this is pertinent to the aim of creating more personalised education. The quality of the education experience does seem to be critical to how students engage, not necessarily through having greater choice over options but through a more engaging educational experience in general. The opportunities for students to raise their voice are limited in almost all countries and where these opportunities exist they are not always seen as effective but depend on the commitment of the teachers, which differs widely. When asked, many students do not wish to have a say over curriculum or the bigger issues of school policy but instead want a school culture where they are respected and they are listened to on issues that very directly concern them. Rather than demanding greater choice they demand a more engaging education, which involves them more in whatever they are learning. If they don't get it, then it may well be seen as useful to have choice options which allow the exercise of "exit".

Regarding research, the findings on satisfaction suggest that our understanding of satisfaction and what it means for students needs to be more multi-dimensional. We need to understand both the learning aspects of schooling and the social context in which it takes place. Such research needs to go beyond the classroom to embrace the culture and climate of a school including the opportunities it offers for meaningful interaction with peer groups. It will be important to distinguish these two aspects in research on satisfaction to be able to address the results which are difficult to interpret at present. Why are older students less satisfied? Is it because learning at a younger age is less overshadowed by the pressure to get high marks or is it because schools fail to offer the right social environment for older students? The same can be asked regarding gender: are girls happier because they are more ambitious when it comes to schooling or is the social environment of schooling more suitable to girls? Or should we look for other ways of looking at these issues, which nevertheless maintain the student learner in spotlight?

To learn about students' expectations and satisfactions is not just interesting for research's sake. In the absence of effective means to make their voice heard, it is through other means (like surveys) that they are giving feedback. If policy is increasingly oriented towards recognising "choice" and "voice" as the legitimate expression of demand, it would be very partial to ignore what the pupils and students themselves have to say while listening to others. It does not seem that students are demanding anything radically different – a frequent complaint to be heard from older generations indeed is how conventional young people are, perhaps a sign that they have grasped all too well how critical educational success can be to their futures. Yet, if educational systems were to answer these criticisms and create active participatory teaching and learning environments and material viewed as interesting and relevant by the students this would imply radical change for many schools and teachers. The power of the student message is enhanced precisely because it is not radically at odds with what systems are officially striving to achieve.

References

Aszmann, A. *et al.* (2003), "11–18 éves tanulók egészségmagatartásának nemzetközi vizsgálata", Kézirat, Állami Népegészségügyi és Tisztiorvosi Szolgálat.

Beňo, M. and T. Beňová (1994), "Rodičia súčasnej škole" (part I.), *Technológia vzdelávania* II, No. 1.

BT (2003), BT Citizenship Research Summary 2003.

CBOS (2002), *Do czego przygotowują absolwentów polskie szkoły średnie?* (What do Polish upper secondary schools prepare their graduates for?)

Central Council for Education (1997), *The Model for Japanese Education in the Perspective of the 21st Century* (First Report).

Children's Council (2002), *Medbestemmelse i folkeskolen* (Co-determination at Folkeskolen), Children's Council, Denmark.

Children's Council (2003), *Dialog på tværs – børn og voksne i øjenhøjde* (Cross dialogue – children and adults at eye level), Annual Meeting of the Children's Council 2002, Children's Council.

Centro de Investigaciones Sociológicas (CIS) (2003), Sondeo sobre la juventud española, *http://www.cis.es*

Department for Education and Skills (DfES) (2004), "Statistics of Education, Schools in England 2004", TSO, London.

Hallgarten, J. and T. Breslin (2003), "Power to the Students", *Times Educational supplement*, 5 September, available: *http://www.tes.co.uk*.

IEA (1999), Výchova k občanství a demokracii (IEA's Civic Education Study).

IEA (2003), PIRLS 2001, "International Report: IEA's Study of Reading Literacy Achievement in Primary Schools".

IEA (ÚIV for the Czech Republic) (1999), *Výchova k občanství a demokracii* (IEA's Civic Education Study).

IFES – Institut für Empirische Sozialforschung (2003), *Bildungsmonitoring*, Research reports commissioned by the Ministry of Education, Science and Culture, Vienna.

Jacobsen, B. *et al.* (2004), *Den vordende democrat* (The future democrat). Magtudredningen (Power report), Aarhus Universitetsforlag, Denmark.

Japan Youth Research Institute (2002), *the Survey on the Future Prospect among Senior High School Students.*

Keele University Centre for Successful Schools (2004), *Annual Attitudinal Survey Data* (private communication).

Keys, W. and C. Fernandes (1993), *What do Students Think about School?*, A report for the National Commission on Education, NFER, Slough, United Kingdom.

Keys, W., S. Harris and C. Fernandes (1995), *Attitudes to School of Top Primary and First-year Secondary Students*, NFER, Slough, United Kingdom.

Konarzewski, K. (2001a) (ed.), *Szkolnictwo w pierwszym roku reformy systemu oświaty* (Schools in the first year of the education system reform), ISP.

Konarzewski, K. (2001b), "Drugi rok reformy strukturalnej systemu oświaty: fakty i opinie" (The second year of the structural reform: facts and opinions), ISP.

Koulutusbarometri (1995), "Helsinki: Opetushallitus ja Suomen Gallup Oy" (Education Barometer 1995. Helsinki: National Board of Education and Suomen Gallup Oy).

Koulutusbarometri (1996), "Helsinki: Opetushallitus ja Suomen Gallup Oy" (Education Barometer 1996. Helsinki: National Board of Education and Suomen Gallup Oy).

Koulutusbarometri (1997), "Helsinki: Opetushallitus ja Suomen Gallup Oy" (Education Barometer 1997. Helsinki: National Board of Education and Suomen Gallup Oy).

Lannert, J. (2004), *Pályaválasztási aspirációk*, Ph.D. dolgozat, BKÁE, Budapest, Hungary.

Malcolm, H., V. Wilson, J. Davidson and S. Kirk (2003), "Absence from School: A Study of its Causes and Effects in Seven LEAs" (Research Brief 424), DfES, London.

MORI (2002), "School Omnibus 2001-2002 (Wave 8). A Research Study among 11-16 Year Olds on behalf of the Sutton Trust", available: *www.suttontrust.com.*

MORI (2004), "School Omnibus 2004 (Wave 10). A Research Study among 11-16 Year Olds on behalf of the Sutton Trust", available: *www.suttontrust.com.*

Morris, M., J. Nelson, M. Rickinson, S. Stoney and P. Benefield (1999), *A Literature Review of Young People's Attitudes towards Education, Employment and Training* (Research Brief 170), DfES, London.

NHK (2002), Public Polls, Japan.

NOP Consumer (2003), *Children and Young People Survey: Summary of Results.*

Ombudsman (2003), *Informe: La escolarización del alumnado de origen inmigrante en España: análisis descriptivo y estudio empírico*, Vol. I and Vol. II, Madrid.

O'Keeffe, D. (1993), "Truancy in English Secondary Schools: A Report Prepared for the DfE", HMSO, London, cited in Morris, M., J. Nelson, M. Rickinson, S. Stoney and P. Benefield (1999), *A Literature Review of Young People's Attitudes towards Education, Employment and Training* (Research Brief 170), DfES, London.

OECD (2003), *Student Engagement at School. A Sense of Belonging and Participation. Results from PISA 2000*, OECD, Paris.

OECD (2005), "How Well do Schools Contribute to Lifelong Learning?", *Education Policy Analysis – 2004 Edition.*

OECD (2006), *Personalising Education*, OECD, Paris.

Park, A., M. Phillips and M. Johnson (2004), *Young People in Britain: The Attitudes and Experiences of 12-19 year olds* (Research Summary), DfES, London.

Provazníková, H. *et al.* (2003/2004), *Spokojenost českých dětí se školou.* (Children satisfaction with school), Učitelské listy, č. 6, pp. 10-11.

Public Agenda (1997), *Getting By: What American Teenagers Really Think About Their Schools.*

Shaw, M. (2004), "It's Getting so Much Better all the Time", *Times Educational Supplement*, 10 September.

Straková *et al.* (2002), *Vědomosti a dovednosti pro život. Čtenářská, matematická a přírodovědná gramotnost patnáctiletých žáků v zemích OECD* (Knowledge and skills for life. Literacy, mathematic and science literacy amonng the 15-years-old students in OECD countries), ÚIV, Prague.

WHO (1998), *Mládež a zdraví* (The Health Behaviour in School-Age Children).

Chapter 6
THE DEMAND DIMENSION:
CONCLUDING ISSUES AND DIRECTIONS

This chapter brings together the different themes explored in the chapters of the report in a concluding discussion. It develops some of the overarching issues that have arisen across this analysis as a whole. These cover the following themes: schooling as more choice driven with more room for "exit"; voice as a priority issue in determining the nature of schooling; generally positive satisfaction levels and what this means for change; particular problems with secondary education; improving deficient intelligence about demand; and fundamental issues arising from the diversity of demands, especially those related to values. The chapter then locates this study in the broader "Schooling for Tomorrow" body of analysis, including the recent report on personalisation. It shows both how this report informs and is informed by this related analysis. The concluding section presents a selection from the many issues identified in this study as warranting further research, national and international.

Introduction

This chapter brings together the different themes explored in the chapters of the report in a concluding discussion. The report has explored different components of the demand dimension in schooling, while acknowledging aspects of demand it has not addressed. Empirical analysis is a key element of the approach taken but the nature of the evidence drawn on and the sketchy knowledge base in many countries mean that the evidence compiled has been used more to illustrate the main issues identified than to chart developments. The report has first presented a conceptual and historical overview, and then used the framework developed to discuss public and parental perceptions regarding schooling. This is followed by exploration of the expression of demand primarily by parents, through "choice" and through "voice", before turning to the student perspective.

This concluding chapter develops some of the overarching issues that have arisen across this analysis as a whole. It is not intended to be a summary, which can be found at the beginning of this report. The chapter then locates this study on demand in the broader "Schooling for Tomorrow" body of analysis and in particular the two most recently-published reports (OECD, 2006a and b). It shows both how this report informs and is informed by this related analysis. The concluding section presents a selection from the many issues identified in this study as warranting further research, national and international.

Selected issues arising

Schooling: more choice driven, more room for "exit"

This report has confirmed the long-term trend noted in the earlier OECD/CERI choice review (Hirsch, 2002). This observed that the notion of "choice" and the situation in which many families exercise an active choice over which school a child should attend, rather than taking it for granted that it will be the local one, have become a more-or-less permanent feature of education systems. This can be described, following Hirschman (1970), as the exercise of "exit". Exit strategies cover a range of different behaviours. They may be as different as parents selecting a private school for their child or students remaining absent from a class they find boring. Based on the systems looked at for this study, most offer parents the choice between public and private provision and most make provisions for the establishment of schools based on private initiative, including in recognition of value choices and beliefs. Opportunities for choice between different schools, within the public system and between public and private provision, have become the rule rather than the exception.

The equity concerns about increasing choice opportunities are familiar. This report does not permit any systematic assessment of different choice arrangements against equity criteria. But, it does confirm that better educated, middle-class parents are more likely to avail themselves of choice opportunities and send their children to the "best" school they can find. This can increase inequalities by widening the gaps between the sought-after schools and the rest. Inequalities widen too because when the most critical parents take their children from the local school, it loses the critical resource of those who tend to be the movers and shakers, *i.e.* those with most effective voice for improvement from within. There are equity arguments, on the other hand, in favour of transparent choice when this means extending to all the same room to choose as privileged parents have always exercised, implicitly or explicitly. In addition, there are the familiar quality arguments in favour of creating greater choice as a vehicle for stimulating improvement. When choices exist, schools must then look beyond their own walls at what others – their potential "competitors" – are doing; without some room for exit to be exercised, parents and students have no threat to back up voice.

How to find the balance between exit and voice, quality and equity? An important part of the answer will be where an education system is to start with. The PISA analyses have usefully classified systems in terms of their aggregate achievement of equity and quality valuably to show *inter alia* that the most successful systems are able to achieve both simultaneously. In this framework of analysis, we can propose that systems with high equality but low quality may well benefit from an injection of strategies which permit exit behaviour and choice while those with high quality and low equality may be suffering from a surfeit of such strategies. This is not a matter to be decided in the abstract as so much depends on cultural factors and recent policies which have led to a country's current position in attaining equity and quality. It is to propose that the competing arguments over the costs and benefits of exit strategies play out quite differently in a system with high attainments and very wide disparities from one where the opposite prevails.

Voice: a priority issue in determining the nature of schooling

It is a matter of definition whether the increasing opportunities in some countries for groups of the population to create the sort of education they want – based on philosophical, religious, or ethnic grounds – should be understood as about choice or voice; it is both. The creation of diversity through different kinds of schools following particular group demands represent some of the most powerful examples of voice being exercised in education today. But they are also among the most controversial. To what extent should different socio-cultural groups regard themselves as sharing universal values and life-chances via the education system? Or should they be able to pursue their own understandings of what these should be? As outlined in Chapter 1, OECD countries are moving into relatively uncharted territory which has recast relationships between supply and demand in schooling.

"Supply-dominated" schooling is characterised first and foremost by lack of opportunity for external voice to be heard. There are plenty of examples in this report to suggest that this is the norm not the exception. It can lead to a further "vicious circle" where low parental involvement reinforces negative views from the education side that parents and the community should have only a very limited say in what goes inside schools, who rightly perceive that schooling is not open to external influence. But there does not seem to be any signs that parents want to run schools themselves, except in extreme cases of exit (such as home schooling). And, those systems where parents already exercise a high degree of voice are likely to be those where there is greatest trust in schools and teachers as the professionals responsible for education. Expanding voice in education is thus more about finding a new balance between supply and demand than about the one displacing the other.

The opportunities for students to raise their voice are limited in almost all countries and where these opportunities exist they are often regarded as ineffective and dependent on the commitment of the teachers, which differs widely. This ineffective student voice coexists with the strong emphasis on citizenship and values in education in many countries, with concerns about low interest and participation by young people in civic life. The question then arises whether the organisation as opposed to the content of schooling is in line with the promotion of democratic values. At the same time, students themselves seem less to identify the formal say in school decision-making as their preferred form of voice as compared with being recognised as active participants in the teaching and learning. And their expectations of schooling tend to be largely conventional so that giving students greater voice would not open the floodgates to fundamental conflict with the aims of schools themselves.

Satisfaction levels generally satisfactory – demand pressures for change?

A possibly surprising finding that comes up throughout this report is the generally high levels of reported satisfaction, though with some notable exceptions. There is a stronger belief in the value and achievements of schooling than many might expect. In many places, education is a higher public priority than other calls on the public purse. Parents with children going to school tend to be satisfied with the education their children receive and are more satisfied than other parents and the public. Again, the message is generally positive, as knowledge of or experience with education leads to higher levels of satisfaction. The general perceptions of school by students are broadly positive albeit with non-academic aspects being most appreciated and with a larger or smaller minority of students who plainly hold negative assessments.

We have outlined a framework for placing the discussion of the demand side of the equation in the interplay between expectations and satisfaction, proposing that genuine dissatisfaction will grow in proportion to the mismatch between perceived realities and initial expectations and that this dissatisfaction is a motor for change. Hence, the generally positive assessments can be read as a sign of endorsement and not as pressure for reform. There are nevertheless other factors discussed in this report with which to qualify this rosy assessment.

First, it is commonplace for the same parents and citizens to be positive about their local school and concerned about the state of education in general. Media, public and political dissatisfaction can co-exist with generally positive satisfaction levels among parents and students. Second, the groups who are typically the drivers of change – the educated middle classes – tend both to be less satisfied but also to have done best with the system as it is. Their concerns may thus be under-estimated by the overall satisfaction measures but the demands themselves will not necessarily add up to an agenda for radical change. Instead, they may be conservative in the sense of wanting first and foremost to safeguard educational privileges. Hence, third, it is inaccurate to think of the supply side as inherently conservative even if this might well describe certain school systems; indeed, perhaps paradoxically, much "demand" pressure on school systems still comes from national, state or local policy makers. Finally, fourth, the diverse group demands based on articulate linguistic, religious or philosophical grounds, as well as the strongly voiced demands from parents of special needs students, do clearly represent motors for change in ways which cut across the standard yardsticks of social background.

What is the problem with secondary education?

There are clear differences in the ways in which primary and secondary schooling are judged by both students and parents. Parental involvement in school life falls between the primary and secondary stages across countries as different as Finland, Hungary, England and Spain. Older students are more critical about schooling than younger ones with primary school children more satisfied than students in secondary schools. In all the countries covered, students in the higher educational tracks tend to be more satisfied than students in vocational education. Enjoyment of learning and engagement in schools decreases with age, and serious disaffection is most marked among secondary students.

Are these patterns only to be expected and explicable in terms of such factors as the onset of puberty or the greater distance from home of many secondary schools compared with the local community primary schools? Do the growing stakes of educational success as studies advance and the beckoning choices regarding higher education and the labour market necessarily reduce enjoyment? Or might it be that too often secondary education is insufficiently "demand-sensitive" and instead excessively dominated by the requirements of administrators and teachers? The focus on demand and the evidence brought together for this study suggest that there may well be in some countries problems of parental and pupil engagement that is open to reform. At the least, these differences between primary and secondary schooling invite clarification.

Improving deficient intelligence about demand

This review has shown the value of exploring this area and of making the evidence base more robust. If education systems wish to be both more "demand-led" and more "evidence-based", this is a terrain where there is much work to do in terms of data collection and of developing mechanisms for feeding the results into the broader debate and decision-making process. This becomes the more important when education systems are not ready to put their faith primarily on market and quasi-market mechanisms as the vehicles through which "demand" is expressed. However, the problems with market mechanisms as the primary vehicle for educational improvement and decision-making are well-known and largely confirmed by this report, particularly in terms of equity of outcomes and the limited number of stakeholders whose voice finds expression.

Hence, improved intelligence – via barometers, surveys, targeted research, and indeed the more standard tools of "consumer research" such as focus groups – can provide important information to all who are involved in education. It will never "speak for itself" nor can decisions be based on pursuit of popularity *per se*. It is rather a useful additional weapon in the armoury of decision-making in systems increasingly seeking to be more "demand-sensitive".

Fundamental issues – moving away from the technocratic view

Chapter 1 distinguishes between individual and collective voices in demand to ask about how far particular community demands should be met through the school system. Such a deceptively simple question raises some of the most controversial issues arising in schooling today. The diversity of demands, as David Plank underlines in his analysis prepared for this study (2005), is now rocking the equilibrium of many school systems and in ways whose outcomes cannot be readily predicted. How far is the school about system-wide integration of all populations and nation-building, part from any specific academic ambitions? Or else should it be the crucible for the recognition, even cultivation, of difference? Is school *par excellence* a secular institution or a legitimate place for the expression of religious beliefs? More generally, what is education for and within that the specific role of the formal public school? Enhancing sensitivity to parental and community demands goes straight into these fundamental questions.

We would not pretend that these questions had disappeared in educational debates and are only now resurfacing. Rather, an enhanced role for and the diversity of demands move the spotlight on from the complicated but contained set of goals to do with improvement, efficiency and equity seen as within the control of "the system" and open to technocratic solution. Education authorities are now in a much more complex situation as regards the making of policy. On the one hand, the growing research and knowledge base fosters the expectations that policies should be evidence-informed. Simple brews of hunch and ideology are not adequate foundations of policy. On the other hand, the greater room for local decision-making (the supply side) and the growing pressure to recognise diverse demands about what education is for means that mechanistic approaches of levers and planned designs become increasingly unattainable. The expectation of being able to control change grows just as the means to do so move out in myriad directions. The demand dimension is both an expression and a cause of this new complexity.

Demand and related "Schooling for Tomorrow" analyses[1]

The overarching trends and dynamics

The fundamental issues discussed above are integral to the two overarching trends proposed by Saussois (2006). These are, first, the development of educational systems from more societal to more individual orientations; second, the movement from closed and bureaucratic systems towards more open systems characterised by a new professionalism (see Figure 6.1.)

---

[1] The recently-published "Schooling for Tomorrow" volume on educational futures thinking (2006b) contains an analysis by Jean-Michel Saussois which is framed in terms of demand and supply. It is both relevant for and informed by this volume. The other recently-published "Schooling for Tomorrow" report on "personalisation" (OECD, 2006a) is particularly related to the issues covered in this volume. Personalisation has arisen at different points in the preceding discussion; indeed, it can be characterised in terms of the responsiveness of the learning provision – the "supply" – to the manifold demands coming from learners and their families.

Figure 6.1. A framework to address the dynamics of educational change: demand and supply

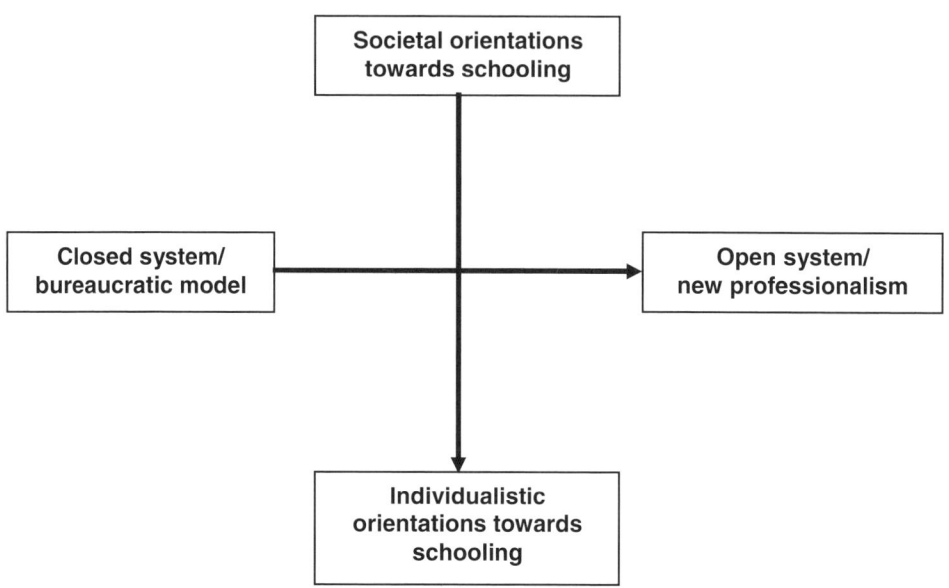

Source: Based on Saussois (2006).

The proposed framework consists of two axes. The "demand" (or "values") axis is about what societies – including families, communities and young people – expect of schools. One polarity of this axis is where there is a strong *societal* orientation for education, with schools central as players in the collective projects of establishing cohesion, equity and social reproduction. At the other end of this axis, schools express a strong *individualistic* orientation, and are very mindful of their "clients" – students and their parents – as consumers. For Saussois, the central role of schools in reproducing social norms is increasingly under scrutiny – by interest and religious groups most obviously but even just parents disappointed by what is on offer and who want to educate their own children with their own values. These groups challenge the legitimacy of schools regarding social values and even knowledge. This trend is about the decline of the idea of national education as an institution: parents expect a service delivery to fulfil their child's needs and whether this is met privately or publicly is not of primary concern.

The "supply line" axis refers to the system as a recognisable entity with different types of resources as inputs and out of which come products or services. Saussois describes this as the axis of closed to open systems. At one end, educational services are delivered within *closed systems* – the rules, methods, criteria for success and so forth are determined in ways largely impervious to outside influence. At the opposite end, they are delivered within an *open system*: there is much greater variety of means in producing a given outcome, calling for considerably more organisation and management in a much more complex operation. The autonomy of schools in an open system allows initiatives coming from both inside and outside. Curriculum and programme options do not only emerge from the supply side (such as teachers proposing electives in subject matter they are familiar with), but from a negotiation of all the stakeholders with a range of different interests in and demands for schooling.

Another way of describing this "supply" axis is as that between highly *bureaucratic* systems, on the one hand, and much more open and flexible ones defining new forms of *professionalism*, on the other. As with demand, Saussois proposes that the broad underlying trend is towards more open forms of professionalism. Not all would agree with the inevitability of the trends in these directions and it remains an open question how far along either axis a current school system may be described.

However characterised, the issues covered in this report can be recast into this framework. The diversification of demand is consistent with the movement down the "demand" axis. There is both a more informed consumerism at play, in education and in public services generally, and there are stronger voices for group demands to be heard. The discussion of this report also suggests that countries are in very different places as regards the movement along the "supply" axis away from bureaucratic closure. Those systems where voice is most problematic – resentment in schools of "external interference", ineffective partnerships with parents and the community, or weak system-wide consultation on programmes – correspond to the characterisation of closure on the left-side of the diagram. *A priori* the trends towards greater choice and diversity suggest a shift towards more openness and new forms of professionalism. However, depending on the powers maintained by the centre, and whether the provision created through diversification is traditional or innovative, choice and diversity might as much describe a shift towards greater individualism and consumerism (moving down the figure) as a move to more open systems marked by a new professionalism (*i.e.* moving left to right in the diagram).

Still more recently, Mortimore[2] brought up the issue that giving greater opportunity for "demand" to be expressed was likely to change the aims of education and left room for two possible responses. First, greater demand sensitivity could change the aims because parents are likely to choose more instrumental ends and the already-advantaged would seek to preserve the advantages they currently enjoy. Second, it is possible that the well-established aims related to quality, preparation for adult life, and equity will survive intact and that the more recent aims are entirely in tune with the wishes of most parents *e.g.* learning to learn more effectively. He regards both as visible in the current situation so that actual outcomes will depend importantly on policy choices. He suggests that policy makers should seek to "hold the line" – balancing individual rights and societal needs. It means endeavouring to cope with "demand" before reaching the tipping point where the affluent and advantaged families opt for private schooling, thus leaving the public system for the disadvantaged and undermining the aim of an equitable society.

Demand and the personalisation of education

There are strong links between personalisation and the issue of "open professionalism". A major question for the personalisation agenda is whether it is possible to have a more demand-led, open system while at the same time recognising the national and broad aims of education. For some, personalisation is essentially individualistic while offering the promise in its more radical definitions to blur and integrate the two sides of the demand and supply equation. Bentley and Miller offer the notion of mass "co-creation" of education where producer and user come together and "the user (learner) is directly involved in both the design and the creation of the learning experience and outcome" (Bentley and Miller, 2006, p. 117). This begs the questions both of how equipped schools are to realise such a vision – how far already along the axis towards open professionalism – and of whether this can ever be a mass phenomenon.

It also raises critical equity issues. Some advocates are more cautious in the sense of recognising how far issues of equality of opportunity and equity intertwine with the potential gains from personalisation. "The more that personalised learning promotes self-provisioning, the more it could widen inequalities (...) The more that services become personalised, then, the more that public resources will have to be skewed towards the least well off to equalise opportunities." (Leadbeater, 2006, pp. 112-113). This report has

---

[2] During the International OECD/Flanders Seminar on "Demand, Autonomy and Accountability in Schooling" held in Brussels in May 2006 to which Mortimore was chief rapporteur.

accepted that choice and voice can operate in tandem rather than necessarily in opposition to each other. But, while it does not go so far as Leadbeater in proposing that personalisation will fail without a very active public policy strategy for equalisation, this is clearly a major risk. Following the dictates of "demand" will not be enough; there is a key role for policy and "supply" to play in addressing the different advantages and disadvantages of the key stakeholders.

The state of knowledge and issues for future research

This study has shown the sketchy nature of the evidence on demand existing as a general rule across countries (though some, such as the Nordic countries, organise regular attitude surveys). If demand is to have an impact on the educational system or on individual schools it will be important systematically to collect information and data on it. This will need to go beyond satisfaction only, which refers to existing schooling practices and so would significantly limit the reform horizon to the already-familiar.

What needs to be better understood therefore are the expectations that parents have, what it is they find important, and what they want from schooling. These are more difficult questions to answer, but they are an important means of bolstering the demand side in systems which tend to be "supply-dominated". It will not be enough just to improve knowledge about parent and student expectations, key stakeholders though they are. Employers, teachers and local communities, for instance, all have important stakes in schools and could become still more important as the missions of schools are widened. We have also stressed that it is not enough to *produce* such knowledge but also to develop processes for how best to *use* it.

As well as more systematic data to feed into policy and decision-making, there is need for research to analyse the complex nature of demand. This study has recognised its multi-dimensional nature. Demands are not just focused on the learning aspects of schooling but on the social aspects too, and these two are interrelated. Parents not only want the best learning outcomes for their children but they also want their children to flourish in the social context which the school provides. Research should focus on both; it needs to look beyond the classroom to include the culture and climate of the school.

Analysis should also help inform understanding of the impact of the move from supply- to demand-driven educational systems. This study identifies a number of potential negative, even vicious, circles and equity problems associated with promoting demand. As far as possible these potential problems need to be underpinned by empirical analysis. This involves looking not only at immediate impacts but widening the focus to the mid- to long-term effects on the educational system and society as a whole. What are the trade-offs between quality gains and equity losses in promoting different forms of choice? How capable are teachers and schools to open their doors and classrooms to wider view and are there tradeoffs in this case with professional trust? What would the consequences be of listening and responding to student voice particularly about the quality of teaching and learning? On these and similar questions, the evidence base could be considerably improved.

For international comparative purposes it will be important to combine quantitative evidence on the achievement levels of students, such as collected through the OECD/PISA surveys, with a deeper understanding of the structures, processes and practices in the different countries being compared. It would be valuable to know to what extent shifting to less centrally-run, demand-led systems contributes to the achievement levels of students and this requires a detailed understanding of the systems that are being compared. Successful policies need to be understood in the context in which they are successful, because the context may be as important – through interaction with the policy being implemented – as the policy itself; simply copying one or two of the elements of the Finnish system, for instance, is not a recipe for success.

Earlier in this chapter we presented the juxtaposition of two overarching trends regarding the demand for and supply of schooling: on the one side, a posited shift from an agreed universal social mission towards a more disaggregated, consumer-driven orientation; on the other, from a bureaucratic, closed system to a more open one based on new forms of organisation and professionalism. Research could usefully refine and chart these major changes taking place, providing operational measures to capture these major sea-changes if indeed they are taking place. This study has made a contribution to this analysis through the lens of improving our understanding of the demand dimension. It is thus situated in the broader current of "Schooling for Tomorrow" analysis which will continue to chart these waters.

References

Bentley, T. and R. Miller R. (2006), "Personalisation: Getting the Questions Right", *Personalising Education*, OECD, Paris, Chapter 8.

Hirsch, D. (2002), "What Works in Innovation in Education, School: A Choice of Directions", CERI Working Paper, OECD/CERI.

Hirschman, A.O. (1970), *Exit, Voice, and Loyalty: Responses to Decline in Firms, Organizations, and States*, Harvard, United States.

Leadbeater, C. (2006), "The Future of Public Services: Personalised Learning", *Personalising Education*, OECD, Paris, Chapter 7.

Miliband, D. (2006), "Choice and Voice in Personalised Learning", *Personalising Education*, OECD, Paris, Chapter 1.

OECD (2006a), *Personalising Education,* OECD, Paris.

OECD (2006b), *Think Scenarios, Rethink Education*, OECD, Paris.

Plank, D. (2005), "Understanding the Demand for Schooling", Report to the OECD.

Saussois, J-M. (2006), "Scenarios, International Comparisons, and Key Variables for Educational Scenario Analysis", *Think Scenarios, Rethink Education*, OECD, Paris, Chapter 3.

Annex
The framework of questions for the country reports

1. Demand and views about schooling in society

> **How does demand feature in educational debate, how are schools regarded by society, and how well are expectations met?**

This section seeks to clarify whether and how the notion of "demand" features in public debate on education in each country, and more generally how schooling is regarded in the public arena, especially the media. It also addresses "demand" through the ways that schools meet or not the expectations of society at large and of different groups within society (parents specifically are the focus of Section 2). It seeks to draw together survey evidence relating to views on education, distinguishing between different aspects of education (priorities, satisfaction levels) and different groups in society (defined in such terms as political affiliation, age, gender, and cultural and ethnic background). It will also be useful to know how, if at all, these views contrast with those held by teachers and school leaders.

Commentary may usefully be added on the broad context of debate on public services. Commentary might also refer to the robustness of the surveys referred to and if/how the results of such surveys are used.

Questions:

- *1.1* Does the notion of "demand" feature in policy discourse and public debate in your country? How commonplace is it now to propose that schooling should be more "demand-sensitive" – by whom, and what is that taken to mean? How important are the distinctions between "social", "individual", and "private" demand?

- *1.2* Have studies addressed changes in the way schools and education in general are presented and discussed in the media? What do such analyses show about the nature of public debate on education?

- *1.3* What is known about how society values the different aims of education? Are there major differences between different sections of society, defined in terms of political affiliation, age, gender, and cultural and ethnic background? What evidence is there to suggest how society in general, and different groups in society, believe that these aims are achieved?

2. The attitudes and expectations of parents

> **What do parents expect of schools and how satisfied are they?**

This section addresses "demand" through the views of a pivotal section of society with demands to make on schooling – parents. It addresses issues of satisfaction with schools, as well as perceptions of what they are for and how well they meet their goals. It also focuses on particular groups of parents, and whether the functioning and outcomes of schooling is perceived to be fair. Where the question refers to "different groups of parents", these are distinguished in terms of criteria such as age, socio-economic status, cultural and ethnic origin. If data permit, it may be useful to distinguish between mothers, fathers, and other close family members; single parents and those living together. Where possible, distinguish between primary and secondary schooling.

Questions:

- *2.1* What is the evidence relating to levels of expressed parental approval of/satisfaction with what is achieved by:

    a) schools in general;

    b) those which their children actually attend.

- *2.2* What evidence exists on the priorities held by parents in general, as well as different groups of parents, about the main aims of schooling and on how well they assess that these priorities are actually achieved? Is anything known about parental satisfaction with the demands made on their children by the school system?

- *2.3* Is there any basis to the assertion that parents tend to the conservative as regards their children's education? Is anything known about the extent to which parents regard schools as a "public good" or instead as a "private consumer good"?

- *2.4* How well do particular groups of parents feel they are served by the school system? How equitable do different groups of parents believe the system to be – in general and in relation to their own children?

3. Participation in decision-making in the schooling process

> How open to external influence is decision-making in schooling – in local
> governance and day-to-day influence – and who exercises such influence?

This section addresses "demand" through the room for local influence over schooling, by students' families and others in the community other than those on the educational "supply-side". This section covers decision-making related to day-to-day influence over the education of the young and to involvement in the general management of schools. It also addresses the sometimes controversial issue of the exercise of parental choice over which school children attend. Attention should be given both to the extent of such influence and, where possible, differentiate between the characteristics of those who exercise it, in such terms as socio-economic background, ethnic and cultural origin, position in the community and residence.

Questions:

- *3.1* What light does research shed on the *level* of involvement of parents and other members of the community in the directions taken by schools in the:

    a) day-to-day directions taken for the education of different classes and pupils;

    b) local governance of schools as institutions?

- *3.2* Are there clear *patterns* relating to which groups of parents or other members of communities tend most to be involved and which least involved, and in what kinds of decision-making? What does the evidence show about *who* exercises available choices over school enrolment (Question 5.2 relates to legislative and constitutional entitlements rather than how this is exercised in practice)?

4. Pupil choices and values

> What do we know about the aspirations and expectations of young people
> themselves, and how well these are met through schooling?

"Demand" here is addressed through evidence of what young people themselves want and aspire to – as revealed by their behaviour and their own reports – and how this aligns with what schooling provides. Any study of "demand" must take account of the views of children and young people but this is not to suppose that such evidence is simple to interpret ("demands" may be inconsistent or ill-formulated, and demand-sensitivity cannot be equated simplistically with either a curriculum "smorgasbord" or "edutainment"). Choices made by young people may as much reflect parental or social influence as their own attitudes. Where available, the findings should be reported on different sections of the pupil/student population – by *e.g.* age; gender; urban/rural; social, cultural or ethnic background.

Questions:

- **4.1** What do young people think about their schooling – its relevance and quality? What is known about what motivates them to study, in particular the balance between intrinsic interest and seeking extrinsic reward? How do the views of young people match with the views of others, including their parents and teachers, about what is important in education?

- **4.2** What are the rates of absenteeism from compulsory school and how does this vary from the beginning of the primary cycle to the end of the lower secondary cycle? What are the characteristics of those who are most persistently absent? Is there evidence about boredom among the young?

- **4.3** What is the room for students and their parents to choose different programmes of study, and how far are these primarily in the hands of schools and the education authorities? How far do young people participate in the decision-making of schools? Is anything known about such influence or participation by young people in any of different types of schools referred to in 5.1?

5. Diversity in the structure of school systems and influence over the curriculum

> **How diversity of demand is recognised in the "supply" of schooling and how broad is the influence over the contents of formal school education?**

This section addresses how different forms of demand are recognised at the system level, both in terms of structures and in terms of influence over the formal content of schooling. It will also provide valuable contextual information through which to interpret the findings reported in the previous sections. This section addresses the breadth of influence over curriculum contents. It also asks for information on areas other than disciplinary and knowledge fields, in particular how values, citizenship and religious education are treated in curricula, hence relating to certain "demands" from the broader society or from particular groups within it. The greater room to exercise choice over the type of school a young person attends is not automatically assumed here to be an indicator of demand-sensitivity, and other questions provide detailed information through which to qualify the material reviewed here.

Questions:

- *5.1* What formal distinctions, if any, are there between types of school distinguished in terms of such factors as ability/selectivity of the student intake, public/private, religious affiliation, or specialisation based on linguistic or curriculum grounds? What is the scale of participation in private schooling and what does "private" mean? Is "home-schooling" legal and under what conditions? Where such alternatives exist, what proportions of the child and youth cohorts are involved in each?

- *5.2* What are the legal/constitutional possibilities for the exercise of choice by parents and students, as regards attendance at, or foundation of, the different types of school described in 5.1, or enrolment at different public schools of the same type?

- *5.3* In what way, if at all, are groups representing civil society and parents involved in defining the school curriculum? Is their influence on curriculum guidelines and the contents of schooling significant?

- *5.4* Are values explicitly treated in curriculum guidelines and in what way? Is there explicit reference to citizenship/citizenship education? To different philosophical or religious beliefs?

Also available in the CERI collection

www.oecdbookshop.org

OECD PUBLICATIONS, 2, rue André-Pascal, 75775 PARIS CEDEX 16
PRINTED IN FRANCE
(96 2006 07 1 P) ISBN 92-64-02840-4 – No. 55327 2006